Royal Society of Victoria

Transactions of the Royal Society of Victoria

Vol. III. Part I.

Royal Society of Victoria

Transactions of the Royal Society of Victoria
Vol. III. Part I.

ISBN/EAN: 9783337163044

Printed in Europe, USA, Canada, Australia, Japan

Cover: Foto ©ninafisch / pixelio.de

More available books at **www.hansebooks.com**

ROYAL SOCIETY OF VICTORIA.

1891.

Patron:
HIS EXCELLENCY THE EARL OF HOPETOUN, G.C.M.G.

President:
PROFESSOR W. C. KERNOT, M.A., C.E.

Vice-Presidents:
E. J. WHITE, F.R.A.S. | J. COSMO NEWBERY, B.Sc., C.M.G.

Hon. Treasurer:
C. R. BLACKETT, F.C.S.

Hon. Secretaries:
H. K. RUSDEN, F.R.G.S.
PROFESSOR W. BALDWIN SPENCER, M.A.

Hon. Librarian:
JAMES E. NEILD, M.D.

Council:

R. L. J. ELLERY, F.R.S.
G. S. GRIFFITHS, F.R.G.S.
A. W. HOWITT, F.G.S.
JAMES JAMIESON, M.D.
A. H. S. LUCAS, M.A., B.Sc.
PROF. ORME MASSON, M.A., D.Sc.

H. MOORS.
PROF. H. LAURIE, LL.D.
PROF. R. T. LYLE, M.A.
ALEXANDER SUTHERLAND, M.A.
C. A. TOPP, M.A., LL.B.
A. S. WAY, M.A.

TRANSACTIONS

OF THE

ROYAL SOCIETY OF VICTORIA.

VOL. III. PART 1.

1891.

CONTENTS.

A MONOGRAPH OF THE VICTORIAN SPONGES, BY ARTHUR DENDY, D.Sc., F.L.S., FELLOW OF QUEEN'S COLLEGE AND DEMONSTRATOR AND ASSISTANT LECTURER IN BIOLOGY IN THE UNIVERSITY OF MELBOURNE.

PART I. THE ORGANISATION AND CLASSIFICATION OF THE CALCAREA HOMOCŒLA, WITH DESCRIPTIONS OF THE VICTORIAN SPECIES. (With Plates I.-XI.)

MELBOURNE.

PUBLISHED FOR THE ROYAL SOCIETY
BY THE SPECTATOR PUBLISHING COMPANY LIMITED, 270 POST OFFICE PLACE.

JULY, 1891

It has been decided by the Council to devote Volume III. of the Transactions to the publication of Dr. Arthur Dendy's Monograph of Victorian Sponges. This forms the first part, and succeeding parts will be issued from time to time.

A MONOGRAPH OF THE VICTORIAN SPONGES, BY ARTHUR DENDY, D.Sc., F.L.S., FELLOW OF QUEEN'S COLLEGE AND DEMONSTRATOR AND ASSISTANT LECTURER IN BIOLOGY IN THE UNIVERSITY OF MELBOURNE.

PART I.—THE ORGANISATION AND CLASSIFICATION OF THE CALCAREA HOMOCŒLA, WITH DESCRIPTIONS OF THE VICTORIAN SPECIES. (With Plates I.—XI.)

(Read December 11, 1890).

TABLE OF CONTENTS.

	PAGE.
I.—INTRODUCTION	2
II.—THE ORGANISATION OF THE CALCAREA HOMOCŒLA	5
A.—THE OLYNTHUS TYPE	5
B.—THE HISTOLOGY OF THE CALCAREA HOMOCŒLA	6
C.—THE CANAL SYSTEM OF THE CALCAREA HOMOCŒLA AS ILLUSTRATED BY THE VICTORIAN SPECIES	23
D.—THE CANAL SYSTEM OF THE CALCAREA HOMOCŒLA IN GENERAL	37
III.—THE CLASSIFICATION OF THE CALCAREA HOMOCŒLA	39
IV.—DESCRIPTIONS OF THE VICTORIAN SPECIES OF CALCAREA HOMOCŒLA	45
HOMOCŒLA SIMPLICIA	45
HOMOCŒLA RETICULATA	49
HOMOCŒLA RADIATA	66
DOUBTFUL SPECIES	69
V.—DESCRIPTIONS OF PLATES	72

I.—INTRODUCTION.

It is now nearly three years since the Port Phillip Biological Survey Committee of the Royal Society of Victoria placed in my hands for the purposes of investigation the splendid collection of sponges dredged by Mr. J. Bracebridge Wilson in the neighbourhood of Port Phillip Heads. Since that time Mr. Wilson has yearly added to the collection, which now numbers nearly two thousand specimens, and is certainly one of the finest collections of sponges in the world.

In dealing with so large a mass of material the first thing necessary was to roughly sort out the specimens into their main groups. In order to accomplish even so much it was necessary to make many hundreds of microscopical preparations, and this preliminary work alone has already occupied a very considerable amount of time.

Meanwhile I wrote to the Natural History Department of the British Museum and asked for fragments of all their Australian sponges for purposes of comparison and identification. Dr. Günther, F.R.S., the Keeper of the Zoological Department of the Museum, responded to my request in the most liberal manner, and I have to offer him my most sincere thanks for sending me several hundred named specimens of Australian sponges, which are of the greatest value in determining the identity or otherwise of the various species in the Port Phillip collection with those previously described by other writers.

I am also greatly indebted to Sir Frederick M'Coy, F.R.S., who has most kindly placed at my disposal all the sponges in the National Museum at Melbourne; to Mr. J. Gabriel for a number of valuable specimens dredged by him chiefly at Westernport (Victoria); to Professor W. Baldwin Spencer, M.A., for the valuable advice which he has always readily given on difficult points; to the Rev. Walter Fielder, for assistance in making microscopical preparations, and above all to Mr. J. Bracebridge Wilson, M.A., Head Master of the Church of England Grammar School, Geelong, for the great majority of the specimens and for several opportunities of accompanying him on his dredging trips and seeing the sponges in the living condition as they first come from the water.

I must also not omit to mention my indebtedness to the Council of the Royal Society of Victoria, who readily agreed to my suggestion that a special volume should be devoted to the monograph on the Victorian sponges, thus enabling the work to appear ultimately in the form of a separate publication instead of being scattered in a series of isolated papers through the Transactions of the

Society. It is hoped that this plan of publication will render the work much more easy of reference to students. It will probably be a long time before the volume is completed, as the work can only be undertaken in the intervals between other duties.

It is proposed to complete the examination of the collection systematically, group by group, and to publish the account of each larger or smaller group as soon as it is completed.

The present contribution contains the account of the simplest and most lowly organised group of sponges, the Calcarea Homocœla. Considerable difficulty was experienced in working out this group owing to the very serious imperfection of our knowledge of the anatomy of these sponges. There appears to be a general idea that the Calcarea Homocœla are all very much alike one another in organisation, and that such small differences as may exist are scarcely worthy of investigation. Hæckel, indeed, in his famous Monograph of the Calcareous Sponges, recognises several distinct types of canal system, but he seems to regard them more as " sports " than anything else, and illustrates them all from what he considers to be a single species (*Ascandra reticulum*).* I do not consider that there is any sufficient evidence in favour of such an extraordinary variation in canal system within the species as Hæckel imagines. Of course the whole difficulty turns upon the question, " What is a species ? " and this is a question which no man can presume to settle off-hand. Whatever else a species may be, however, there can be no doubt that such a thing has no existence in Nature, the term being used by zoologists and botanists merely as a matter of convenience to indicate a group of individuals which resemble one another to a certain extent.† If, however, we are going to place in one and the same species forms so widely divergent in anatomical characters (canal system) as those which Hæckel places in his *Ascandra reticulum* we might as well do away with the term altogether.

Von Lendenfeld has added two types of canal system to the Calcarea Homocœla, for which, while accepting Hæckel's views as to the intra-specific variation of the canal system in other forms, he creates two new families, *Homodermidæ and Leucopsidæ*. The former are supposed to be a transition form between the Asconidæ and Syconidæ, and the latter between the Asconidæ and Leuconidæ. The mania for discovering (or inventing) " connecting links " has probably done an immense amount of harm to the progress of biological science. If zoologists would be content to describe what they see in a straightforward manner, instead of going out of their way to discover connecting links, the study of zoology in general and of spongology in particular would be greatly facilitated.

---

* "Die Kalkschwämme." Vol. 3, Plate 20.

† This question is further discussed later on, in the section dealing with the classification of the Calcarea Homocœla.

The descriptions* given by Dr. von Lendenfeld both of *Homoderma* and *Leucopsis* are so inadequate and the specimens upon which the two new "families" are based avowedly so minute, that I cannot help feeling considerable hesitation in accepting them without further evidence. In thus refusing to accept Dr. von Lendenfeld's *Homodermidæ* and *Leucopsidæ* without further evidence I am only following the example of so eminent a spongologist as Dr. Vosmaer.†

These considerations have induced me to pay particular attention to the minute anatomy of the Calcarea Homocœla, and my researches have shown that in the more highly organised forms the canal system becomes far more complex than has been hitherto believed, leading to a complexity of organisation amongst the Homocœla perhaps equal in degree, although different in kind, to any found at any rate amongst the Sycon *Heterocœla*. Moreover my observations support those of Dr. von Lendenfeld in that I have found a type of canal system closely agreeing with that of his *Homoderma*, but in a totally distinct species (*Leucosolenia tripodifera*, Carter sp.) of such a size and represented by so many specimens that mistake is impossible.

In working out the Calcarea Homocœla I have been much aided by the kindness of Mr. H. J. Carter, F.R.S., the well-known English writer on sponges. Some years ago Mr. Bracebridge Wilson forwarded large collections of sponges to Mr. Carter, by whom they were described in a series of papers in the "Annals and Magazine of Natural History," the types being afterwards lodged in the British Museum. Thus many of the species with which I shall have to deal in this monograph have already been described by Mr. Carter, but the descriptions are brief, without illustrations, and the anatomy is scarcely touched upon. Thus it becomes a matter of great difficulty to recognise many of them, but this difficulty in the case of the Calcareous sponges has been to a large extent obviated by the kindness of Mr. Carter, who sent me a copy of his work with numerous manuscript illustrations and unpublished notes. For this and numerous other acts of kindness I must express my hearty thanks to Mr. Carter.

Type specimens of the sponges described in the present work will be deposited in the Biological School of the Melbourne University, and it is proposed also to send a set to the National Museum in Melbourne and to the British Museum in London.

* Proceedings of the Linnean Society of New South Wales, Vol. IX., Part 4., pp. 1088, 1089.
† Bronn's "Klassen und Ordnungen des Thierreichs." "Porifera," p. 387.

II.—THE ORGANISATION OF THE CALCAREA HOMOCŒLA.

A.—THE OLYNTHUS TYPE.

In the hope that the present work may be of use to naturalists, and especially Australian naturalists, who are not professed spongologists, I propose to deal more in detail with the anatomical side of the question than would otherwise be necessary, and to commence by describing briefly what may be regarded as the simplest and most typical form of organisation met with in the group. We may then investigate the more readily in what manner and to how great an extent the other members of the group differ from this typical form.

The simplest type of organisation met with in the group is known by Hæckel's term "*Olynthus*",[*] and this name may conveniently be retained for the type of organisation in question, though not as indicating a "genus" in the ordinarily accepted meaning of that term.

In the Olynthus type, then, the sponge consists of a small, thin-walled tube or sac, the lower end of which is closed and attached to some foreign object, while at the upper end is a large opening known as the *osculum*. The wall of the tube, moreover, is perforated by numerous very minute apertures known as the inhalant pores or *prosopyles*.[†] The prosopyles, the cavity of the tube (*gastral cavity*), and the osculum together constitute what is known as the *canal system* of the sponge, here met with in its simplest condition.

The wall of the tube is made up of three distinct layers. On the outside is a single layer of flattened, plate-like, nucleated epithelial cells, polygonal in shape and in contact with one another at their edges; this layer is known as the *ectoderm*. On the inside is a single layer of "collared cells" known as the *endoderm*, and between the endoderm and ectoderm is the *mesoderm*, consisting of a layer of gelatinous material in which are embedded the skeleton of the sponge (consisting of calcareous spicules) and various kinds of cells.

The histological characters of these three fundamental layers will be described in detail later on, meanwhile it is important to remember that these three layers are found in all sponges and that they always exhibit the same essential characteristics, although numerous differences in detail are met with.

---

[*] "Die Kalkschwämme," Vol. 1, p. 219 *etc.* Vol. 3, Plate 1, Fig. 1.

[†] The term "prosopyle" is used by Sollas, in his article on Sponges in the "Encyclopædia Britannica," to designate the openings of the inhalant canals into the flagellated chambers and to distinguish them from the inhalant pores on the surface of the sponge. In a thin walled Olynthus the inhalant pores and prosopyles are so close together that they may for all practical purposes be regarded as identical. In higher forms, however, it is very convenient to have distinct names for the two structures.

Throughout the life of the sponge a stream of water may be observed issuing through the osculum from the gastral cavity, the water which thus flows out being constantly replaced by smaller streams which flow in through the prosopyles. This stream of water is maintained by the activity of the flagella of the collared cells composing the endoderm.

Such then, in brief, is the structure of the *Olynthus*, which is to be regarded as a single individual or Ascon-person.* No examples of the Olynthus type occur in the collection of Victorian sponges, but for an illustration I would refer students to Hæckel's *Ascetta* (*Leucosolenia*) *primordialis*, admirably illustrated in his Atlas of the Calcareous Sponges.† It is probable that all Calcareous sponges pass through an Olynthus stage at an early period of their life history.

B.—THE HISTOLOGY OF THE CALCAREA HOMOCŒLA.

The Ectoderm.

The true nature of the ectoderm of Calcareous sponges was first elucidated by Schulze in his well-known memoir on the structure and development of *Sycandra raphanus*.‡ Hæckel, in his Monograph on the Calcareous Sponges, had altogether failed to comprehend the true condition of things, and had confused the two layers, ectoderm and mesoderm, under the one name *Exoderm* (used as a synonym for *Ectoderm*). Hæckel states§ that the "exoderm" consists firstly of a "syncytium," and secondly of the spicules. "*Syncytium* nenne ich bei den Kalkschwämmen die ganze Gewebsmasse, welche durch die Verschmelzung der Geisselzellen des Exoderms der Flimmerlarve entstanden ist, mit Ausschluss der darin gebildeten Kalknadeln. Dieses Syncytium ist aus folgenden Bestandtheilen zusammengesetzt : (1) der *Sarcodine*, einer hyalinen, structurlosen, contractilen Grundsubstanz, dem modificirten Protoplasma der verschmolzenen Zellen ; (2) den bleibenden und sich vermehrenden *Kernen* dieser Zellen, und (3) den *Spicula-Scheiden*, welche durch Verdichtung der Grundsubstanz rings um die Oberfläche der Spicula entstanden sind." Hæckel himself, in his latest work on sponges, recognises his error, and acknowledges the correctness of Schulze's view ; to quote his own words : "Three years later (in 1875) this conception was corrected by the accurate observations of Franz Eilhard Schulze, the excellent spongiologist, who has advanced in so many important directions the

---

* We may conveniently retain this term although Hæckel's group name "Ascones" has been abandoned.
† "Die Kalkschwämme," Vol. 3, Plate 1.
‡ "Ueber den Bau und die Entwicklung von *Sycandra raphanus* Hæckel." Zeitschrift f. wissensch. Zoologie, Vol. XXV. Suppl., p. 247.
§ "Die Kalkschwämme," Vol. I., p. 160.

knowledge of this class of Cœlenterata. Employing new methods of histological examination, he discovered on the surface of many sponges a delicate external pavement-epithelium not hitherto observed, and deduced from this observation the following important conclusions :—

"The body of the sponges is originally composed not of two, but of three primitive cell-layers, corresponding to those which in the higher organised Metazoa are called exoderm, mesoderm and entoderm. The exoderm (or outer layer covering the external faces) and the entoderm (or inner layer lining the canal-system internally) are two simple epithelial plates, and between them is enclosed the mesoderm (or the middle layer); this latter is a kind of connective tissue, and produces not only the skeleton, but also the sexual cells (eggs and sperm).

"The conception of the sponge-tissues given by F. E. Schulze is now generally accepted, and it is very probable that it has general value, though it was not possible to demonstrate clearly in all sponges the delicate exodermal epithelium."*

The Calcisponge in which Schulze discovered the ectodermal epithelium was *Sycandra raphanus*, one of the *Heterocœla*. It was of course tolerably safe to assume that a similar ectodermal layer exists also in the *Homocœla*, but I am not aware that this has hitherto been definitely proved. Poléjaeff,† indeed, gives a figure of a section of *Leucosolenia poterium* in which what are evidently intended for ectodermal cells appear, but the figure is very diagrammatic, and there appears to be no mention of the ectodermal cells anywhere in the letterpress.

As a matter of fact I find that the ectoderm of the Homocœla agrees precisely with what Schulze has described for *Sycandra raphanus*, and what I myself found and described in *Grantia labyrinthica*.‡ Except in the case of very well preserved specimens it is a matter of great difficulty to make out satisfactorily the structure of the ectodermal epithelium. In cases, however, where the specimen has been at once immersed in a sufficient quantity of strong spirit and the sections carefully prepared by means of the paraffin method, care being taken to avoid overheating, the ectoderm generally appears in section as a delicate but sharp outline with a moniliform or beaded appearance due to the swelling caused by the presence of the nucleus in the centre of each cell. In my sections of *Leucosolenia wilsoni*, n. sp., for example, I found the ectoderm unusually well preserved. In sections vertical to the plane of its extension it presented the appearance described above (Pl. VII., Figs. 2, 3), but where it happened to be cut tangentially, or sliced off, its true character could readily be seen (Pl. VII., Fig. 4). It consists of thin, flattened, plate-like cells,

---

* Report on the Deep-Sea Keratosa of the "Challenger" Expedition, p. 13.

† Report on the Calcarea of the "Challenger" Expedition, Plate 3, Fig. 1.

‡ "Studies on the Comparative Anatomy of Sponges, III.—On the Anatomy of *Grantia labyrinthica*, Carter, and the so-called Family Teichonidæ." Quarterly Journal of Microscopical Science, January, 1891.

polygonal in outline, and each with a swelling in the centre where the nucleus is situate. The cell itself averages about 0·0136 mm. in diameter, and the nucleus, which is very distinctly outlined and more or less spherical (or perhaps somewhat flattened in the same manner as the cell), has a diameter of about 0·0034 mm. Within the nucleus appear a few small, deeply staining granules. Around the nucleus the protoplasm is highly granular, exactly as described by Schulze, while towards the periphery of the cell it becomes gradually hyaline. Adjacent cells are in contact at the edges, and all together form a single-layered, continuous epithelium over the outside of the Ascon-tube. As a rule, in ordinary preparations, although the nuclei and granules of the ectoderm cells may be clearly enough visible, it is very difficult to distinguish the outlines.

Von Lendenfeld[*] observes: "The whole outer free surface of the Sponge is covered with a low Epithelium, consisting of flat covering cells, each of which may possess one swinging cilia." This author habitually figures cilia on the ectodermal cells both of calcareous and non-calcareous sponges, and it would be interesting to know if he has actually seen them or merely assumed their presence, perhaps from observing currents in the surrounding water. It does not seem to me probable that the ectodermal cells of the Calcarea Homocœla are ciliated.

The Endoderm.

According to Hæckel[†] the cells (termed by Sollas "choanocytes" and by Carter "spongozoa," but generally known as "collared cells") of which the endoderm in the Calcarea Homocœla is entirely composed are so uniform in structure, not only amongst the Calcareous sponges but also in other groups, that the description of one species will serve for all. Until recently this has been the general view and it has become customary with some spongologists to figure the collared cells in their drawings like so many bricks in the plan of a building, apparently without taking the least trouble to investigate for themselves the true state of the case. No one can suppose, for instance, that Polèjaeff ever saw the collared cells in the not too well preserved material at his disposal anything like so plainly or so regularly arranged as he figures them in his Reports on the Calcarea and Keratosa of the "Challenger" Expedition. The structure of the collared cells having been made out by James-Clark,[‡] Carter,[§] Hæckel[||] and Schulze[¶] in a few cases, it was assumed that all collared cells were the same, and

[*] Proceedings of the Linnean Society of New South Wales, Vol. IX., Part 2, p. 318.
[†] "Die Kalkschwämme." Vol. I. p. 137.
[‡] "Spongiæ ciliatæ, as Infusoria flagellata." Memoirs of the Boston Society of Natural History, Vol. i. Part 3, 1867.
[§] "Notes Introductory to the Study and Classification of the Spongida." Annals and Magazine of Natural History. Ser. 4, Vol. xvi., 1875.
[||] "Die Kalkschwämme," loc. cit.
[¶] Loc. cit.

spongologists seem to have thought themselves justified in figuring them in what was considered to be the orthodox manner whether they had been able to make out the structure or not. Certainly they were tolerably correct as to what may be called the typical form of the collared cell, and before passing on to describe the various modifications which have been shown to exist by more independent investigation we may with advantage describe the structure of this typical form.

Typically, then, the collared cell consists of a rounded or sometimes cylindrical body produced above into a neck or collum. The neck is surmounted by a long, vibratile, whip-like flagellum, and the flagellum is surrounded by a very delicate, transparent, membranous collar which is usually more or less funnel-shaped and is inserted on the collum around the base of the flagellum. In the body of the cell is a large nucleus, provided sometimes, if not always, with a distinct nucleolus. The protoplasm around the nucleus is more or less granular and sometimes contains, according to James-Clark, Carter and Hæckel, one or more contractile vacuoles. Both collar and flagellum appear to be capable of complete retraction and in this retracted condition the collared cells are generally met with in sections. According to Carter[*] the collared cell (spongozoon), after removal from the body of the sponge, may be seen moving about the field of the microscope in the form of an *Amœba*, with or without the flagellum. It is not improbable that the amœboid phase may also occur normally within the sponge. For further details and excellent figures I may refer the reader to the works of James-Clark, Carter, Hæckel, and Schulze last quoted.

In his article on Sponges in the "Encyclopædia Britannica" (Ed. IX.), Sollas first showed that in some Tetractinellid forms a peculiar modification of the collared cells occurs, and he gives further details in his Report on the "Challenger" Tetractinellida. This modification consists in the fusion of the margins of the collars of adjacent collared cells in such a manner as to form a distinct membrane, stretching from collar to collar and perforated by circular apertures through which the flagella project. Soon after this I discovered the same membrane very clearly shown in a horny sponge (Carter's *Stelospongus flabelliformis*), and proposed[†] for it the name "Sollas's membrane." Bidder also mentioned[‡] its existence in Calcareous sponges, a discovery confirmed by myself in the case of *Grantia labyrinthica*.[§] So far, however, no one had been able to see both Sollas's membrane and the flagella of the collared cells co-existent, but since then I have very clearly seen both at once in

---

[*] *Loc. cit.*
[†] "Studies on the Comparative Anatomy of Sponges, II.—On the Anatomy and Histology of *Stelospongus flabelliformis*, Carter; with Notes on the Development." Quarterly Journal of Microscopical Science, December, 1888.
[‡] Proceedings of the Cambridge Philosophical Society, Vol. VI., Part 4, p. 183.
[§] "Studies on the Comparative Anatomy of Sponges, III.," *loc. cit.*

preparations of the siliceous sponge *Halichondria panicea*.* For more detailed descriptions and illustrations of this remarkable modification of the collared cells in certain sponges I must refer the reader to the writings of Sollas and myself just quoted.

Sollas, again,† has pointed out that in the calcareous sponges the collared cells are usually, if not always, larger than in other sponges, a statement which is supported by my own observations. According to Haeckel, the collared cells in the Calcarea range from 0·005 to 0·009 mm. in diameter, while in the non-calcareous sponges Sollas gives the diameter of the collared cells as only 0·003 mm.

Enough has been said to show that the collared cells are not so uniform in structure in all sponges as has generally been supposed, and I must now make a few observations on the condition of these elements in the Calcarea Homocœla.

We have seen above that the collared cell is a more or less polymorphic structure, and this polymorphism is exhibited mainly in a great readiness to withdraw the collar and flagellum into the protoplasmic body of the cell. The mere act of removing a sponge from the water and placing it in alcohol seems, as a rule, to be sufficient to cause the total retraction of the collars and flagella, and it is in this condition of retraction that the collared cells are generally found in microscopical preparations. Even in this state, however, they are readily recognisable. Exactly as the ectodermal cells form an epithelial membrane over the outside of the Ascon-tube, so the endodermal, collared cells form a continuous epithelium lining the inside of the tube. For the sake of clearness this lining of collared cells is coloured red in all the figures. When looked at from above or below this epithelium presents the appearance shown in the red-coloured portion of Figure 5, Pl. VI. It consists of a number of retracted collared cells lying side by side. The individual cells are small, in *Leucosolenia cavata*, for example, measuring about 0·0085mm. in diameter. They usually appear more or less polygonal from mutual pressure, although at the same time, owing, doubtless, to shrinking caused by the action of reagents, they generally stand a little apart from one another in the sections, so that the outline of each is distinctly visible. The nucleus of each cell is generally clearly visible; in *Leucosolenia cavata* its diameter is only about half that of the cell itself. The collared cells, and especially the nucleus, stain deeply with the ordinary staining fluids, such as Borax Carmine and Kleinenberg's Hæmatoxylin, and are thus rendered very conspicuous in stained preparations. The usual appearance of the collared cells, when seen in sections taken at right angles to the surface which they cover, is shown in Figure 4, Pl. VI.

* "Studies on the Comparative Anatomy of Sponges, IV.—On the Flagellated Chambers and Ova of *Halichondria panicea*." Quarterly Journal of Microscopical Science, January, 1891.
† Article "Sponges." Encyclopædia Britannica, Ed. IX.

In many cases the collared cells appear to be but very feebly attached to the underlying layer of mesoderm, and frequently they come away over large areas in the course of preparation. Hence, sometimes, they cannot be found at all.

Occasionally, however, the collared cells are exceptionally well preserved and only partially retracted, even in ordinary sections prepared by the paraffin method. This is the case in one of my preparations of *Leucosolenia proxima*. Figure 3, Pl. VIII. shows three collared cells placed side by side in a row, and each one exhibits the characteristic collar still expanded. The collars are funnel-shaped or tubular, and come into contact at their margins, without, however, forming a distinct Sollas's membrane. Of course in the case of collars which thus come into contact at their margins, a temporary fusion may take place as between any two naked masses of protoplasm, and in this manner Sollas's membrane in all probability first arose. Between the bodies of the cells, filling up the interstices, a transparent substance is seen, which is probably part of the gelatinous ground substance of the mesoderm in which the bodies of the collared cells are partially embedded. Figure 4, Pl. VIII. shows another collared cell from the same preparation which has become entirely separated from the rest of the sponge and yet distinctly exhibits its tubular collar. None of these cells show the flagellum, which always seems to be retracted before the collar. The transverse diameter of the body of the collared cell is, in this species, scarcely 0·005mm., while the length of the body and collar taken together is 0·013mm.

Even in the small group of the Calcarea Homocoela at least one interesting deviation from what may be regarded as the typical condition of the collared cells is found, and probably more will subsequently be shown to occur when the subject receives the attention which it deserves. The peculiarity to which I now refer occurs in the very remarkable species *Leucosolenia tripodifera*, Carter sp., and is illustrated by Figures 5 and 6, Pl. VIII. In the first place there is a well-developed Sollas's membrane in the ordinary position. The flagella of the cells are retracted, but the collars are in some cases well preserved and funnel-shaped. Their margins do not come into direct contact, but are united by the membrane, which runs from one to another at right angles to the long axes of the collars. In vertical sections this membrane appears as a thin, sharp line running parallel to the row of collared cells, and at a little distance (about the length of a collared cell body) from it (Fig. 6). Not only, however, is Sollas's membrane present, but it presents in itself a very peculiar modification. Instead of being perfectly smooth the outer surface is thickly studded with delicate, rod-like processes of uniform length and projecting at right angles from it into the gastral cavity. These processes are about 0·007 mm. in length and 0·0012 mm. in diameter; they stain lightly and have a distinctly granular appearance; they are arranged with great regularity and occur in specimens from different localities, so that they would appear to be of constant occurrence in the species. From their general appearance one is at first tempted to imagine that they are bacilli, but their constancy and peculiar and regular arrangement argue strongly against this view. If, on the other hand, we suppose that Sollas's membrane serves to catch or filter food particles from the streams of water flowing through the sponge, as maintained by Bidder and myself, then it seems possible that the curious rod-like processes in *Leucosolenia tripodifera* may be a further device for the same purpose. Such, at any rate, is the only explanation which I can offer of their presence, although I freely admit that it is far from being proved to be the correct one.

The Mesoderm.

The mesoderm consists of a gelatinous ground-substance in which are embedded the spicular skeleton and various cell-elements.

The Ground-Substance.[*]—This is usually but feebly developed in the Calcarea Homocœla. It is doubtless of an inter-cellular nature and formed probably as a secretion of certain of the cells embedded in it, though to which of these cells it owes its origin we cannot with certainty say. Hæckel, indeed, says[†] that " it is secreted by the connective tissue cells of the mesoderm, which are derived originally from the primary exoderm cells," and this view is probably correct. In the Homocœla, and, indeed, so far as we at present know, in all the Calcarea, the ground-substance is clear and transparent and destitute of the numerous granules so characteristic of many horny sponges (*e.g.*, *Stelospongos flabelliformis*). Upon the extent to which the ground-substance is developed depends the thickness of the mesodermal layer. In some species, *e.g.*, *Leucosolenia lucasi* (Pl. IV., Fig. 1) the mesoderm forms a very thin and inconspicuous layer. In others, however, such as *L. stolonifer* (Pl. VI., Fig. 1), *L. cavata* (Pl. VI., Fig. 4) and *L. wilsoni* (Pl. VII., Figs. 2, 3), it is much more strongly developed and forms a layer of considerable thickness. Immediately around each spicule the ground substance is concentrated in the form of a delicate " spicule sheath," visible as a distinct structureless membrane when the spicule itself is dissolved out by means of weak acids.

The Mesodermal Cell-Elements.—The different kinds of mesodermal cell-elements as yet recognised in the Calcarea Homocœla are as follows :—

(1.) The ordinary multipolar or *Stellate Connective Tissue Cells* are the most abundant.

In *Leucosolenia stolonifer*, for example (Pl.VI., Figs. 1, 3), these cells, though very small, are easily visible and plentiful. Each consists of a small, deeply staining,

---

[*] "Maltha" of Hæckel. Report on the Deep-Sea Keratosa of the "Challenger" Expedition, p. 15.
[†] *Loc. cit.*

spherical nucleus, about 0·0025 mm. in diameter, around which is aggregated a small body of granular protoplasm running out in various directions into long, thread-like processes. Adjacent cells are united together by these processes so as to form a network, as in higher sponges. Similar cells are shown in the case of *Leucosolenia cavata* on Pl. VI., Figs. 4, 5.

We may mention here a very remarkable development of the stellate connective tissue cells which takes place in *Leucosolenia proxima*. In this sponge the cells in question, instead of all remaining embedded in the gelatinous ground-substance between the ectoderm and endoderm in the normal manner, have grown out between the collared cells of the endoderm into the gastral cavity, where they form a delicate network, as shown on Pl. VIII., Fig. 2. The cells composing this network are of very large size, but otherwise do not differ from normal multipolar mesoderm cells. They are nucleated and around the nucleus are a number of granules. Some of the protoplasmic processes of the cells retain connection with the mesoderm of the tube-wall, thus supporting the network in the gastral cavity. Such an extraordinary development of the mesoderm seems almost incredible, but it is far too distinct and obvious in my numerous sections of the sponge in question to admit of any doubt; moreover it leads on to a still further development in the same direction in an allied species (*Leucosolenia wilsoni*), which will be fully described in dealing with the canal system.

(2.) The *Amœboid Cells* ("Wanderzellen" of German authors) are difficult to distinguish from the ordinary stellate ones, closely resembling the latter with the long processes cut off. They are somewhat more massive and rounded in outline.

(3.) I am not able to state with certainty whether or not sub-dermal *Gland Cells* occur in the Homocœla. In *Leucosolenia ventricosa*, however, I have found certain elements resembling to a great extent the sub-dermal gland cells described by me* in *Grantia labyrinthica*, but I do not venture to express a definite opinion as to their nature.

(4.) In some cases certain of the mesodermal elements become specially modified to form more or less plate-like *Endothelial Cells*. These occur in two distinct situations and differ in character accordingly. The two kinds of mesodermal pavement cells (endothelial cells) which I have as yet met with in the group are (*a*) the lining cells of the embryo-containing cavities and (*b*) the cells which ensheath the spicule-rays projecting into the gastral cavity.

I have shown elsewhere† that in *Stelospongos* the developing embryos are lodged in special cavities, excavated, as it were, in the substance of the mesoderm, and that

---

* "Studies on the Comparative Anatomy of Sponges, III.," &c. *loc. cit.*
† "Studies on the Comparative Anatomy of Sponges, II.," &c. *loc. cit.*

those cavities are lined by a single layer of gigantic pavement cells whose function appears to be to supply the growing embryo with nourishment. Poléjaeff* had previously called attention to "the extraordinary growth of the endothelial cells surrounding the growing embryos" in various horny sponges. Schulze† long since showed that the embryos of *Sycandra raphanus* lie in special cavities in the mesoderm lined by flattened pavement cells, and I have found the same thing in *Grantia labyrinthica*.‡ But in neither of these two cases do the pavement cells of the embryo capsule exhibit anything remarkable in size or form, as in the horny sponges referred to above. Similar endothelial capsules occur around the ova of *Leucosolenia pelliculata*, but do not require further description.

I have now, however, to record the occurrence, in *Leucosolenia wilsoni*, of embryo capsules composed of large, thick, plate-like cells resembling, though on a smaller scale, those found in *Stelospongos*. The peculiar position of the embryos in *Leucosolenia wilsoni* will be described later on, when we come to speak of the canal system. Suffice it now to observe that they lie in spherical cavities excavated in the mesoderm. The cavity itself is about 0·14 mm. in diameter, and is lined by a single layer of large, polygonal cells of unusual thickness (Pl. VII., Fig. 3). Each cell is about 0·028 mm. in diameter, and 0·009 mm. in thickness. The protoplasm composing it is highly granular and stains well. The nucleus is small and spherical, measuring only about 0·005 mm. in diameter; owing doubtless to the granular nature of the protoplasm surrounding it, it is not easy to make out. There can be no doubt that the function of these cells is to supply the developing embryo with nutriment, but I have not seen any connection between them and the ectodermal cells of the embryo such as I have described in *Stelospongos*.

We have next to deal with the endothelial cells which ensheath the spicule-rays projecting into the gastral cavity. In many Homocœla quadriradiate spicules are present, and the apical ray usually, if not always, projects through the layer of collared cells into the cavity of the Ascon-tube (gastral cavity). Probably in all cases this projecting ray is not naked, but clothed by an investing sheath of flattened, plate-like, nucleated cells. This cellular sheath is very distinctly shown in my preparations of *Leucosolenia stolonifer* (Pl. VI., Fig. 2), and again in *Leucosolenia tripodifera*. If the spicule is dissolved out by means of weak acid, as happens in staining the preparations by the borax-carmine method, the cellular sheath is left as an empty, elongated, conical bag, hanging on to the wall of the gastral cavity. The cells composing the sheath somewhat resemble the cells of the ectoderm, and are arranged like them in a single layer. Their nuclei are very distinct, about 0·0034 mm. in

---

* Report on the Keratosa of the "Challenger" Expedition, p. 52.
† "Ueber den Bau und die Entwicklung von *Sycandra raphanus* Hæckel." Zeitschrift f. wissensch. Zoologie, Vol. xxv. Suppl.
‡ "Studies on the Comparative Anatomy of Sponges, III.," &c. *loc. cit.*

diameter, and stain deeply, but the actual outlines of the cells I have not been able to distinguish. The collared cells of the endoderm are not continued over this sheath, but, as shown in Pl. VI., Figs. 1, 2, cease abruptly around its base. These structures must not be confounded with the ordinary " spicule sheath " always found investing Calcareous sponge-spicules *(vide supra)*. The latter has been shown by Hæckel[*] to be simply a concentration of the gelatinous ground-substance immediately surrounding the spicule, and has no cellular structure.

The origin of the cellular spicule sheaths is open to debate. I prefer at present to regard them as mesodermal structures, but, on the other hand, there is nothing to prove that they are not endodermal. If, however, they are endodermal then Lendenfeld's emended diagnosis of the Homocœla as "Calcispongiæ the entoderm of which consists throughout of frilled flagellate cells,"[†] will no longer hold good. The spicules themselves are certainly mesodermal in origin, and if they can penetrate through the endoderm what is to prevent them from carrying with them an investment of mesodermal cells? Probably these cells are really calcoblasts, which secrete constant additions of carbonate of lime whereby the spicule is enabled to maintain its growth. It is not certain which of the mesodermal cells, as a general rule, function as calcoblasts (*i.e.*, secrete the spicules), but I have elsewhere given it as my opinion that the ordinary stellate connective tissue cells do the greater part of the work.[‡]

(5.) The next mesodermal elements of which we have to speak are the *Reproductive Cells*. Schulze,[§] Poléjaeff,[||] and others have shown that the ova and spermatozoa in Calcareous (and, indeed, other) sponges develop in the mesoderm, and are formed directly from the amœboid cells ("Wanderzellen"). The ovum is formed simply by increase in volume of the amœboid cell and the spermatozoon by a process of fission; for further details of these processes, I must refer to the works of Schulze and Poléjaeff just quoted.

The spermatozoa I have not seen, at any rate in the Calcarea Homocœla, but we may assume that they resemble more or less closely those described by Poléjaeff in *Sycandra raphanus*, consisting of a very minute spherical head and a very long and slender tail (0·03 mm. long).

---

[*] " Die Kalkschwämme."

[†] Proceedings of the Linnean Society of New South Wales, Vol. IX., Part 4, p. 1083.

[‡] In my memoir on the Anatomy of *Grantia labyrinthica* (*loc. cit. supra*) I have proposed to distinguish between two kinds of spicule-secreting cells, or calcoblasts, in the Calcareous sponges, viz., *primary calcoblasts*, within which the spicules take their origin as in mother cells, and *secondary calcoblasts*, which add successive layers of carbonate of lime to the spicule after it has once been formed. I am not aware that anyone has ever yet seen a primary calcoblast, but their existence is rendered probable by the analogy of siliceous sponges, in which the smaller spicules are often seen within mother cells (primary silicoblasts). The ordinary stellate connective tissue cells, or some of them, probably function as secondary calcoblasts, as also do the endothelial cells ensheathing the rays of spicules which project into the gastral cavity.

[§] " Ueber den Bau und die Entwicklung von *Sycandra raphanus* Haeckel." Zeitschrift f. wissensch. Zoologie, Vol. XXV. Suppl.

[||] " Über das Sperma und die Spermatogenese bei *Sycanda raphanus* Haeckel." (" Aus. dem LXXXVI. Bande der Sitzb. der k. Akad. der Wissensch., I Abth, Nov. Heft, Jahrg., 1882.")

The ova, on the other hand, are easily recognisable, and frequently met with in preparations. Figure 4, Plate VI., for example, shows an ovum of *Leucosolenia cavata*, lying in the gelatinous ground-substance of the mesoderm beneath the layer of collared cells. This ovum is simply a very large amœboid cell, about 0.025 mm. in its longer diameter, with an oval form and a very distinct nucleus about 0·006 mm. in diameter. The nucleus is granular, and stains (in this case) more deeply than the surrounding protoplasm, which is also granular. Around this ovum are congregated a number of other mesodermal cells (probably amœboid) of much smaller size. These are probably the commencement of the characteristic capsule which seems generally to surround the developing embryo of calcareous sponges. Possibly the particular ovum here described is not adult, for it does not present quite the characteristic appearance of a ripe calcisponge ovum.

In a specimen of *Leucosolenia pelliculata*, however, I found very numerous mature ova of much more characteristic structure, and these may be taken as a type for the whole group. In this species the wall of the Ascon-tube is very thin, and the mesoderm is but feebly developed. The mature ova, on the other hand, are very large, their shorter diameter measuring two or three times the thickness of the wall of the tube. Hence, wherever an ovum occurs, the tube-wall is swollen out, and the swelling always projects inwards, into the gastral cavity, and not outwards, for the ovum lies inside the layer of rigid spicules composing the skeleton of the sponge. Hence the layer of collared cells lining the gastral cavity is lifted up into a mound-like swelling over each ovum, exactly as I have described in the case of the developing embryos of *Grantia labyrinthica*.* Moreover, the ovum already lies in a distinct cavity lined by a delicate endothelial membrane just like the embryo capsule of *Sycandra raphanus* or *Grantia labyrinthica*.

The ovum itself (Pl. VIII., Fig. 7) is usually irregularly oval in longitudinal section, flattened on the side which lies next to the spicules and swollen out on the other. It measures about 0·085 mm. in longest diameter. The nucleus is very large, and its shape appears to follow that of the ovum to which it belongs; its longer diameter measures about 0·042 mm. in length; it lies pretty nearly in the centre of the ovum. There is always one very large spherical nucleolus whose position in the nucleus varies. It lies sometimes towards one end, sometimes to the side, and in one case I distinctly saw the nucleolus lying half inside the nucleus and half in the surrounding protoplasm. The nucleolus is about 0·01 mm. in diameter. With regard to the more minute structure of these different parts of the ovum we must notice that the body of the ovum (*i.e.*, the part outside the nucleus) is a naked mass of coarsely granular protoplasm which stains very deeply. The nucleus is enclosed in a very distinct

---

* "On the Pseudogastrula Stage in the Development of Calcareous Sponges." Proceedings of the Royal Society of Victoria, 1889, p. 93.

nuclear membrane, which stains deeply, and it is itself composed of a much more finely granular material which stains less deeply than the outside protoplasm. The nucleolus stains more deeply than any other part and appears to be homogeneous and devoid of structure. In addition to the large nucleolus there are generally visible in the nucleus a number of very much smaller bodies resembling the nucleolus in appearance, but it is doubtful whether they have really the same composition as the latter, especially when we compare them with similar bodies in the ovum of *Leucosolenia depressa*, which I propose to describe next.

In my only specimen of *Leucosolenia depressa* adult ova are extremely abundant. Like the embryos in the closely allied species, *Leucosolenia wilsoni*, the ova are imbedded in the mesodermal tissue which in part blocks up the cavities of the Ascon-tubes (gastral cavities), but there is no definite layer of large, plate-like, nutritive cells around each. Such may, however, be formed later on as the embryo develops. The ova are of great size, measuring 0·17 mm. in longer diameter, and, as is usually the case with the ova of the same sponge, are all in very much the same state of development and resemble one another closely. Figure 8, Plate VIII., represents a section of one of these ova. The outline of the section is indicated by the dotted line and, to save labour, only a portion of the protoplasm outside the nucleus is filled in. The ova vary somewhat in shape and may be described as irregularly spherical. Owing to the absence of spicules from the surrounding tissues they are not definitely flattened on one side as in *Leucosolenia pelliculata*. The nucleus is very large indeed, 0·076 mm. in diameter, and approximately spherical. The nucleolus is distinct and also spherical, 0·0085 mm. in diameter. Within the nucleolus several small, highly refringent granules are visible.

The body of the ovum, outside the nucleus, is composed (principally at any rate) of distinct, closely packed, more or less spherical granules, each about 0·003 mm. in diameter; the whole forming a deeply-staining mass. The nucleus is composed as usual of a very finely granular and less deeply-staining substance, and is invested in a very distinct, deeply-staining membrane. Just inside this membrane, and for the most part touching it, lies an irregular row of spherical granules closely resembling in size and other characters the granules of the outer protoplasm. These granules occur in the same position with great constancy in all the ova, and form a characteristic and conspicuous feature. They look as if they were granules belonging to the outer protoplasm which have actually passed through the nuclear membrane. Whether this passage is normal or pathological (due to reagents) I know not. In *Leucosolenia pelliculata* we have already seen similar granules, but they are not arranged with anything like the same regularity around the inside of the nuclear membrane, nevertheless a tendency towards such arrangement may sometimes be observed, as is shown in Figure 7, Plate VIII. In the latter species also I noticed, as described above, the nucleolus itself half in and half out of the nucleus, and this fact supports the supposition that the granules of the outer protoplasm may under certain circumstances pass through the nuclear membrane (in the opposite direction to that in which the nucleolus appeared to be travelling). Another feature of considerable interest in the ova of *Leucosolenia depressa* is the presence in the nucleus of distinct traces of a nuclear network, composed of very delicate, branching and anastomosing threads, which seem to stain more darkly than the surrounding protoplasm, and appear somewhat as shown in the figure.

These examples may suffice to illustrate the structure of the ovum of the Calcarea Homocœla, and indeed, of calcareous sponges in general.* Although the adult sponge is generally admitted to be amongst the simplest and most lowly of organisms, the ovum appears to be possessed of a complexity of structure far beyond what might be expected, and this complexity appears especially to concern the nucleus.

Such then are the various cell-elements which take part in the formation of the mesoderm of the Calcarea Homocœla, but in addition to these there occur in the mesoderm of *Leucosolenia cavata* a great number of bodies whose nature is still a matter of conjecture, but which may be conveniently described in this place.

Yellow Granules.—The bodies in question lie embedded in large numbers and grouped at fairly regular intervals in the mesoderm beneath the layer of collared cells (Pl. VI., Figs. 4 and 5); they consist of spherical granules (perhaps small cells), mostly aggregated in very definite clusters and each with a dark spot in its centre (nucleus ?). The arrangement of the granules in each aggregation is peculiar and characteristic. First they may be arranged in a solid heap of comparatively small size, about 0·025 mm. in diameter. This appears to be an immature condition (Pl. VI., Fig. 5). Sometimes there appears in such a heap a dark area resembling a nucleus, which seems to indicate that the whole mass of granules may be originally a single nucleated cell. Then the granules, each about 0·0023 mm. in diameter, appear to spread themselves out, so that in the next stage, which I regard as the more advanced condition, they form a ring surrounding an empty, discoid or sometimes crescentic space (Pl. VI., Fig. 5). One side of the ring appears to be always thicker (*i.e.*, composed of more granules) than the other, which may be composed of only a single row of granules. The diameter of this annular aggregation of small cells or granules is about 0·034 mm.

* For further particulars as to the ova of sponges *vide* Dendy, " Studies on the Comparative Anatomy of Sponges," III. and IV., *loc. cit.*

The nature of these "yellow granules," as I propose to call them, is extremely enigmatical and the first question which presents itself is, do they really belong to the sponge in which they are found or are they parasitic or symbiotic organisms?

There are two arguments in favour of the view that they really belong to the sponge. (1) They occur in great numbers, arranged in the same manner and having the same characteristic structure in all specimens of *Leucosolenia cavata* that I have examined, so much so as to form one of the most striking characteristics of the species. (2) They bear a rather striking resemblance to the developing flagellated chambers described by me in the embryo of *Stelospongos flabelliformis*.*

On the other hand there are very serious arguments against this view. (1) They are only known to occur in this species and, perhaps, in *Leucosolenia coriacea*† and *L. osculum* (*vide infrà*) (I find them also in *L. dubia* but it is not impossible that that "species" may be a young form of *L. cavata*.) (2) With the exception of the structures already mentioned in the embryos of *Stelospongos flabelliformis* they are unlike any other structures found in sponges, and it is scarcely conceivable that they can be developing flagellated chambers, or masses of collared cells, because the true collared cells in *L. cavata* are plainly visible, altogether different in appearance and distributed in a totally different manner. The idea that they might form a kind of accessory chambers at one time commended itself to me but I can see nothing to warrant such a supposition; moreover the crescentic or discoid space in the centre of the annular group of granules shows no connection with the canal system of the sponge. (3) The behaviour of the granules towards reagents is not altogether what one would expect if they were really sponge-cells. Their colour, when mounted in balsam without staining, is distinctly yellowish. They stain well, however, with hæmatoxylin. When treated with solution of iodine alone, or with iodine and sulphuric acid, no blue colour is discernible, but when fragments of the sponge are boiled in caustic potash solution for the purpose of isolating the spicules the yellow granules withstand the action of the potash and appear in the preparations of the spicules. This last observation leads me to

---

* "Studies on the Comparative Anatomy of Sponges, II. &c." Quart. Journ. Micro. Sci., Dec. 1888 (*vide* especially Pl. XXXIII. Fig. 23.)

† In a paper in the Annals and Magazine of Natural History for July 1884 (pp. 21, 22), Mr. Carter describes certain granular bodies in Bowerbank's *Leucosolenia coriacea* which must I think be of a similar nature to the yellow granules of *Leucosolenia cavata*. He describes them fully, but unfortunately without figures; the description runs as follows:— "Taking the granule singly, it is spherical, translucent, and glairy, glistening from refraction of light, of a faint yellow tinge, and varying under 1·6000th of an inch in diameter, although rarely attaining this size in this state. They are, when *in situ*, congregated round a nucleated cell (the ' Kern ') which is often so indistinct here as to be very difficult to see, owing to its delicate (? polymorphic) structure and the opaque mass which the granules form when closely applied to it in juxtaposition; or they are scattered throughout the syncytium in the same way as in the Foraminifera . . . . . Iodine does not turn them purple, nor does liquor potassæ dissolve them; but strong nitric acid appears to destroy their sphericity, which may be brought back again by the addition of liquor potassæ. This glairy refractive appearance gives them the aspect of fat or albumen; while, like the green granules in *Spongilla*, they appear in the sulphur-yellow and scarlet varieties of *Grantia clathrus   . . . Leucosolenia coriacea*) to be the seat of these colours respectively, when they might be termed 'pigmental.' It is possible that they grow into the larger cells of the protoplasm (the ' Kerne'), from which they appear to be derived, when they may fulfil other offices. . . . . But whatever the office of the granules may be no one as yet has demonstrated beyond conjecture what they are or what purpose they may subserve either in the sponges or in the Rhizopoda,—so they are still called ' the granules.'"

suppose them to be of vegetable nature. The iodine-sulphuric acid test is to my mind by no means a conclusive one, and in spite of my failure to detect starch or cellulose by its means I am inclined to favour the view that these very characteristic and remarkable bodies are symbiotic algæ.

To judge from a passage in Mr. Carter's description of *Leucosolenia* (*Clathrina*) *cavata** and from the fact that the yellow granules occur abundantly in a specimen of that sponge sent by him to the British Museum and thence to me, I think that Mr. Carter must have seen them. The passage referred to runs as follows:—" Structure that above mentioned, whose staple is the 'tubulated thread,' of which the wall is very thin and skeletally composed of a single layer of radiate spicules held together by sarcode supporting the softer parts, which here appear to consist chiefly of a layer of spongozoa in juxtaposition, and not gathered into the form of ampullaceous sacs, *together with a remarkable quantity of those organs which consist of nucleated cells surrounded by an abundance of glistening spherical granules, which Hæckel has figured and named 'nuclei' (Kerne) of his 'Syncytium.'*" The portion of the passage italicised leaves no doubt in my mind that Mr. Carter refers to the yellow granules, but he is probably mistaken in supposing that they have anything to do with the nuclei of Hæckel's "Syncytium." The latter are simply the nuclei of the various cells which compose the ectoderm and mesoderm, and these also are clearly visible in my preparations of *Leucosolenia cavata* (Pl. VI., Fig. 5).

The Skeleton.—Having now discussed all the cell-elements which occur embedded in the ground-substance of the mesoderm, we come next to the skeleton.

The skeleton of all calcareous sponges consists of isolated spicules never united together into fibres or networks as in the siliceous forms. We will first speak of the spicules themselves and then of their arrangement.

The excellent researches of von Ebner† have recently thrown much light upon the physical nature of the calcareous sponge-spicule. According to this author the spicule contains no organic basis, but is a crystalline formation, composed chiefly of calcspar, but with an admixture of other salts :—" Die Nadeln der Kalkschwämme sind hauptsächlich aus Kalkspath bestehende, keine organische Substanz enthaltende Individuen von Mischkrystallen, deren äussere Form—ohne Begrenzung durch wahre Krystallflächen—von der specifischen Thätigkeit eines lebenden Organismus bedingt ist und deren innere Structur, obwohl vollständig krystallinisch, durch eine

---

* "Annals and Magazine of Natural History," June, 1886, p. 502.

† "Über den feineren Bau der Skeletheile der Kalkschwämme nebst Bemerkungen über Kalkskelete überhaupt." ("Aus dem XCV. Bande der Sitzb. der kais. Akad. der Wissensch. I. Abth. März-Heft., Jahrg. 1887.")

eigenthümliche Vertheilung der Gemengtheile mit der äusseren Form in Beziehung steht." The spicules, as already stated, are formed as secretions of certain mesodermal cells, and each is invested by a very delicate organic sheath which is, however, no part of the spicule itself, but simply a concentration of the gelatinous ground-substance surrounding it.

Three, and only three, main forms of spicules occur amongst the Calcarea, and all three occur amongst the Homocœla. They are—(1) The triradiate spicules, which are by far the commonest, and which seem to be the primitive form amongst the Calcarea. (2) The quadriradiate spicules. (3) The oxeote spicules.

Triradiate Spicules.—Each consists of three rays or arms radiating from a common centre. Of these spicules Hæckel distinguishes* three groups—(1) *Regular triradiates*, in which the three angles and the three rays are alike. (2) *Sagittal triradiates*, in which two of the angles, or two of the rays, form a pair, while the third is in some way different. (3) *Irregular triradiates*, in which the three rays, or the three angles, or both, are all unlike. This classification is convenient; but it must be carefully borne in mind that the three types are not sharply defined, but merge insensibly into one another, so that it is often impossible to say, without very exact measurement, to which of the three groups a particular spicule should be referred.

In the simplest cases the rays of the spicule are straight, and generally sharp-pointed at the extremity. Frequently, however, they become more or less curved. The curvature may take place either in the plane of the three rays, as, for example, in the case of many sagittal spicules, where the two paired rays often curve either towards or away from one another; or the rays may curve in such a manner that if the spicule be laid on a level surface it will rest on the apices of the rays only, with the centre of the spicule elevated to a greater or less extent. An excellent example of this latter kind of curvature is shown in the so-called "tripod-spicules" of *Leucosolenia tripodifera* (Pl. XI., Fig. 5). Amongst the Calcarea Homocœla I have frequently noticed that the spicules on the outside of a sponge colony are more robust, and also exhibit a greater degree of curvature than those in the interior (*e.g.*, *Leucosolenia tripodifera*).

In the sagittal triradiates the two paired rays are known as the *lateral* or *oral rays*, the angle between them as the *oral angle* and the unpaired ray as the *basal ray*.

Quadriradiate Spicules.—With Hæckel, I regard the quadriradiate spicule as a derivative of the triradiate, and the fourth ray, which projects from the centre of the spicule in a plane at right angles to that of the other three, as a secondary develop-

* "Die Kalkschwämme." Vol. I., p. 187.

ment. The three primary rays are spoken of by Haeckel as the *facial rays*, and the fourth as the *apical ray*. As in the case of the triradiates the quadriradiate spicules may be classified as regular, sagittal and irregular.

In some species triradiate spicules pass almost insensibly into quadriradiates, the apical ray appearing first as a tiny wart in the centre of the spicule, and only a very few quadriradiates occurring amongst a vast majority of triradiates. Sometimes only one or two quadriradiates can be found in a preparation, and it is quite impossible to be certain, from the mere fact that no quadriradiates at all can be found, that none exist in the sponge. Hence the hopelessness of attempting to classify the Calcarea by their spicules alone or even principally.

Oxeote Spicules (Oxea).—I use this term for the spicules named by Haeckel "*Stabnadeln,*" because they resemble in form the siliceous spicules to which the term "oxeote" was originally applied by Mr. Ridley and myself in our Report on the Monaxonida of the "Challenger" Expedition. The oxeote spicule has only a single axis, and thus consists of a simple rod which, in its most typical condition, is spindle-shaped and pointed at the two ends, which are precisely similar. This typical condition, however, is seldom found. The spicule is nearly always curved, and one end is nearly always of different shape to the other. It appears to me, however, useless to attempt to give special names to all the varieties of oxeote spicules.

Further details as to the forms assumed by the spicules in different species are unnecessary in this place, the nomenclature having been explained I must refer the student for further particulars to Haeckel's monograph and to the systematic portion and illustrations of the present memoir (Plates IX., X., XI.).

With regard to the arrangement of the spicules in the Calcarea Homocœla there are one or two points of general interest which offer themselves for consideration. In the simplest case the skeleton consists of triradiates only, placed side by side with considerable regularity in a single layer in the thickness of the mesoderm. If the spicule be sagittal it is so placed that the lateral rays and oral angle are directed towards the osculum and the basal ray towards the base of the sponge. If quadriradiates be present they appear nearly always to be so placed that the apical ray projects through the endoderm into the gastral cavity, generally curving upwards towards the osculum, and thus affording a protection against the entrance of parasites. If, on the other hand, oxeote spicules be present, they seem always to lie nearer to the ectoderm than either the triradiates or quadriradiates, and very commonly one end, which is usually slenderer and more sharply pointed than the other, projects outwards and upwards through the ectoderm, forming a protection to the outside of the sponge. The position and arrangement of these three kinds of spicules is well illustrated in *Leucosolenia lucasi* (Pl. IV., Fig. 1).

C.—The Canal System of the Calcarea Homocœla as Illustrated by the Victorian Species.

The portion of our subject with which we have now to deal is perhaps the most difficult. We have already described the Olynthus type, and have seen that it consists essentially of a narrow, thin-walled tube, open at one end only. Now the question before us is—Given a narrow tube capable of indefinite elongation and capable also of branching and anastomosing to an indefinite extent, to determine how many different forms the sponge colony resulting therefrom may assume.

It will be seen that under the term "canal system" I include not only the canal system of the individual Ascon-person, but also that of the sponge colony as a whole. This is necessary, for in some cases, as we shall see (*e.g.*, *Leucosolenia cavata*), the individuals of which the colony is composed are so intimately united together that we can no longer disentangle them, and we cannot treat of the canal system of one Ascon-tube without at the same time treating of that of its neighbours; indeed, the individuals no longer have each its own canal system, but the colony has a canal system common to them all. The canal system of the colony is of course determined by the manner in which the individual Ascon-tubes are united together, and hence in describing the canal system we must at the same time describe the form of the colony, and *vice versâ*. In the more complex forms of Calcarea Homocœla it is almost as impossible to recognise individuals as it is in the most highly developed sponges such as the *Keratosa*, and the term canal system is equally applicable, with the same significance, to both.

The Olynthus is the individual unit of the sponge, and must be regarded as a single animal developed directly from a single ovum. It may in fact be compared to a *Hydra*. But the Olynthus has generally, like the *Hydra*, a strong tendency to form buds or branches, but, unlike in *Hydra*, these branches never separate from the parent. They form with the parent permanent colonies, as in such hydroids as *Obelia*. Still we have no difficulty as yet in distinguishing the individuals (Ascon-persons) which compose the sponge colony from one another, each is only connected with its fellows at the base, and each has its own gastral cavity and its own osculum. But now the different members of each colony begin to branch more and more, and to fuse with one another wherever the branches come in contact, communications being established at these points between adjacent gastral cavities. Thus more or less complex networks of tubes are formed, and every chance of distinguishing between the individual "persons" which compose the colony is lost. We only know, from analogy, that the whole sponge is a colony, and not a single individual. In this anastomosis of the different members of the colony to form complex networks, and their consequent loss of individuality, the sponge colony differs widely from the hydroid colony. The connection between the individuals which compose the colony is a far more intimate one than in any other colonial metazoa. The entire colony now behaves as one individual, it has its own characteristic size and shape, its own exhalant openings (*oscula*[*] or *pseudoscula*) and its own inhalant pores (*pseudopores*) and external skin (*pseudoderm*).

We must now describe in detail the principal modifications which the sponge colony, and as a direct consequence the canal system of the colony, present amongst the Victorian Calcarea Homocœla.

According to the modifications in the form of the colony and of the canal system I propose to divide the genus *Leucosolenia*, which with Poléjaeff and Vosmaer I regard as the sole genus of Homocœla, into three sections, *Simplicia, Reticulata,* and *Radiata*. We will deal with these divisions in order, beginning with the least complex.

Section 1. *SIMPLICIA.*

The Simplicia include such simple Olynthus types as never form colonies, and also those colonial forms in which the whole colony consists of individuals (Ascon-persons) which may branch, but which never form complex anastomoses nor give off radial tubes, so that the individuality of the different members of the colony is always recognisable.

As already stated, no species which permanently retain the simple Olynthus form have been met with amongst the Victorian Sponges. The simplest form which we have appears to be *Leucosolenia lucasi*.

This sponge is very minute, the individuals (Ascon-persons) of which the colony is composed measuring only about 2 or 3 mm. in length and 0·7 mm. in diameter. The colony increases by budding, the buds appearing on the parent tube first as blind outgrowths, which subsequently develop each an osculum at its free end. Hence the whole colony forms a loose, branching mass of indefinite size and shape, attached to some foreign object. A portion of such a colony is represented on Plate I., Figure 1.

Each individual tube resembles an Olynthus except that instead of being closed at its lower extremity it remains in open communication with its neighbours. The minute structure of a single individual is shown on Plate IV., Figure 1. It consists of a thin-walled, sub-cylindrical or sometimes nearly conical tube with a wide osculum

---

[*] The osculum of a compound sponge is not strictly homologous with the osculum of an *Olynthus*, but corresponds to a number of *Olynthus* oscula run together.

at its upper extremity. The thin wall of the tube is perforated by numerous circular inhalant pores (prosopyles) placed in the intervals between the spicules and leading directly from the exterior into the gastral cavity. The diameter of the prosopyles in the spirit-preserved specimen is about 0·01 mm. but they may have been a good deal larger in life. (According to Hæckel[*] the inhalant pores [*Tubi porales*] are not permanent structures but appear and disappear again in the living sponge with no regularity. They appear in any part of the tube wall simply by a process of shrinking away of the surrounding soft tissues. The ectoderm appears to be the first part to give way and the endoderm the last. Then they disappear again by a reversal of the process, the collared cells being the last to close in and resume their original position. When they have closed completely no trace is left of their existence. Hence it happens that in spirit-preserved specimens the prosopyles are often not visible ; they are completely closed. In other cases their position is indicated only by gaps in the layer of collared cells, the ectoderm and the mesoderm only having closed in. The diameter of the fully open prosopyles is usually, according to Hæckel, from 0·01-0·02 mm.) The number of the prosopyles is very great, as will be seen by reference to Figure 1, Plate IV.

A slight advance in complexity is exhibited by *Leucosolenia stolonifer*. Here the individual Ascon-persons arise from a creeping, tubular, stolon-like structure (the *spongorhiza*) which spreads over the substratum on which the colony is growing in every direction. The spongorhiza may perhaps be regarded as the parent of the colony, it grows horizontally itself but its buds (the younger Ascon-persons) grow upwards and become much wider in diameter than the parent tube. The parent spongorhiza also produces short downward outgrowths which serve to attach the colony to the substratum on which it grows (Pl. I., Fig. 2). A strong tendency to form a spongorhiza is also exhibited in *Leucosolenia lucasi* but is not so well marked as in *L. stolonifer*. The spongorhiza is comparable to the similar structure (*hydrorhiza*) found in many hydroids.

The upright Ascon-persons of *Leucosolenia stolonifer* resemble those of *L. lucasi* except in their very much greater size and in the greater thickness of the tube wall. They rarely branch or anastomose, and, except when very young, each one is provided with a wide terminal osculum ; the youngest individuals end blindly. When fully grown they attain a height of about 35 mm., and a diameter of about 3·5 mm.; they narrow slightly towards the osculum. Owing to the unusual thickness of the Ascon-tube wall the inhalant pores are somewhat different from those of *L. lucasi*. They are no longer simply circular apertures perforating a thin membrane. The wall of the tube averages about 0·14 mm. in thickness, and its outer surface is extremely uneven. Numerous wide apertures, or depressions, lead into irregular canals in the thickness

[*] "Die Kalkschwämme" Vol. 1., p. 220, *et seq.*

of the wall. These canals, after branching slightly and diminishing greatly in diameter, terminate in small openings (the true prosopyles), only about 0·02 mm. in diameter, which perforate the layer of collared cells (Pl. VI., Fig. 1). The elongation of the inhalant pores into distinct canals is due to the unusual thickness of the mesoderm. Since these canals appear to be lined by an ingrowth of the ectodermal epithelium they are probably more permanent structures than is usually the case with the inhalant pores of the Calcarea Homocœla. Possibly they are capable of opening and closing only at the gastral end (prosopyle) where they perforate the layer of collared cells.

Section II. *RETICULATA*.

In this section of the genus the sponge colony forms a more or less complex network of branching and anastomosing tubes, and it is no longer possible to distinguish the individual Ascon-persons of which the colony is composed.

The canal system presents great variations within the section, and before proceeding to describe individual examples it will be as well to give an outline scheme of the chief types, of which I recognise six, and which I propose to distinguish as types A, B, C, D, E, F of the reticulate form of canal system. These six types of canal system may be arranged in two groups, which I propose to regard as subsections of the Reticulata, and to term *Indivisa* and *Subdivisa* respectively.

Subsection 1. *Indivisa*.

The gastral cavities of the Ascon-tubes composing the colony retain the primitive hollow condition, there being no ingrowth of the mesoderm or endoderm.

Division 1.—The colony forms a loose network of tubes (Ascon-tubes) still well separated from one another, and without a common investing skin (pseudoderm). Hence there are no definite pseudopores.

Type A., with the characters of the division.

Example.—*Leucosolenia dubia*, n. sp.

Division 2.—The colony is formed of tubes (Ascon-tubes) branching and anastomosing in a very complex manner. The whole colony forms a compact mass, and the outer walls of the outer tubes generally become specially thickened and contain specially large spicules, forming a more or less definite investing skin (pseudoderm). This skin is perforated by numerous small apertures, the pseudopores, which communicate with the narrow interspaces between the Ascon-tubes in the interior of the colony. The pseudoderm is also perforated by larger exhalant openings *(oscula* or *pseudoscula).*

> *Subdivision 1.*—The exhalant openings, through which the water leaves the sponge, are true oscula, *i.e.*, they lead directly into a space lined by collared cells and formed by the union of a number of Ascon-tubes.
>
>> *Type B.*, canal system normal.
>>
>>> *Examples.—Leucosolenia stipitata,* n. sp. *Leucosolenia pulcherrima,* n. sp.
>>
>> *Type C.*, canal system reversed.
>>
>>> *Example.—Leucosolenia cavata,* Carter sp.
>
> *Subdivision 2.*—The exhalant openings through which the water leaves the sponge are pseudoscula, *i.e.*, they lead at first into a space not lined by collared cells, but, presumably, by ectoderm. This space is a *pseudogaster,* it really lies outside the colony and is formed probably by the upgrowth of the colony around it. The Ascon-tubes open into the pseudogaster.
>
>> *Type D.*, with the characters of the subdivision.
>>
>>> *Example.—Leucosolenia ventricosa,* Carter sp.

Subsection 2. *Subdivisa.*

The gastral cavities of the Ascon-tubes are more or less subdivided into incomplete chambers by ingrowths of mesoderm, or of both mesoderm and endoderm.

> *Type E.*—The collared cells have not yet spread in over the ingrowths of mesoderm.
>
>> *Example.—Leucosolenia proxima,* n. sp.
>
> *Type F.*—The collared cells have spread in over the ingrowths of mesoderm.
>
>> *Examples.—Leucosolenia wilsoni,* n. sp. *Leucosolenia depressa,* n. sp.

Having thus briefly reviewed the six types of canal system which I have found amongst the Victorian reticulate Homocoela we may pass on to describe somewhat more in detail an example of each.

Type A.—*Leucosolenia dubia* consists of a network of tubes spreading in many planes and varying in the closeness of its meshes not only in different specimens but even in different parts of the same colony. Figure 3, Plate I., represents a small portion of a colony enlarged four times. We cannot of course distinguish the Ascon-persons of which the colony is composed, we can only distinguish between what I propose to call *Ascon-tubes* and *interspaces*. The Ascon-tubes are of course lined by collared cells (endoderm) and the interspaces by ectoderm. Although the interspaces in the outer portions of the colony (and indeed also in the inner portions) are often no wider than the Ascon-tubes themselves yet no definite external skin *(pseudoderm)* is formed, and hence no definite pseudopores. The structure of the Ascon-tube is the same as in the Homocœla Simplicia. It is cylindrical and about 0·5 to 1 mm. in diameter, but varies a good deal in different parts of the same colony. True oscula are occasionally visible on the upper surface of the colony. Two or three Ascon-tubes open by the same osculum and the diameter of the latter is rather less than that of an Ascon-tube. The prosopyles are not visible in my specimens, they are probably closed. As the thickness of the tube-wall is unusually great (about 0·1 mm.) the inhalant pores must be elongated, probably they resemble those of *Leucosolenia stolonifer* described above.

Type B.—The simplest example of this type is afforded by *Leucosolenia stipitata*. The entire colony is only about 8 mm. in height and is perched on the summit of a short stalk. Figures 4, 5, 6, Plate I., show the external form. The colony consists of a network of Ascon-tubes so disposed that there is one main tube running vertically through the centre of the colony, into which the remaining tubes debouch. The main tube is probably not to be regarded as the parent stock from which the others have been budded out but as formed by the fusion of a number of tubes to form a single axial cavity. It is lined throughout by collared cells and ends at the summit of the colony in a single, wide, true osculum. Figure 2, Plate IV., shows a vertical section through the colony, in which the relations of the different Ascon-tubes is made clear. From this it will be seen that the interspaces are necessarily confined to the peripheral portions of the colony. The outer tubes of the colony are very wide and the interspaces between them correspondingly small, hence there is a common pseudoderm formed by the outer walls of the outer tubes, in which the interspaces appear as definite pseudopores (Pl. I., Fig. 6). The pseudoderm is strengthened by spicules of somewhat greater size than those found in the interior of the colony. The walls of the Ascon-tubes are very thin and the prosopyles are very clearly visible in my stained preparations both in the inner and outer tubes of the colony; they are circular apertures about 0·02 mm. in diameter.

Another good illustration of this type is found in *Leucosolenia pulcherrima*, the only point of difference to notice as regards the canal system being the presence of several true oscula instead of a single one, but this character is probably not constant. Figure 7, Plate I., shows the external form of the colony and Figure 3, Plate IV., the arrangement of the canal system.

Type C.—The only example which I know of this very remarkable, reversed type of canal system is afforded by *Leucosolenia cavata*.

This sponge forms large, massive colonies (Pl. II., Fig. 7) which may attain a height of four or five inches (100 or 125 mm.) The colony is characteristically flattened from side to side and also on the upper surface. On the upper surface are a large number of true oscula, each surrounded by a membranous collar (Pl. V., Fig. 1). Between the oscula are a few small pseudopores but the majority of the pseudopores occur on the sides of the colony as little oval openings closely scattered all over the well-developed pseudoderm (Pl. II., Fig. 7).

The lowermost portion of the colony, which is also the oldest portion and the part attached to the substratum on which the sponge grows, consists of a number of well separated, although branching and anastomosing Ascon-tubes. In short, the first-formed part of the colony retains the comparatively simple form of type A (*e.g.*, *Leucosolenia dubia*), except that the Ascon-tubes for the most part grow vertically upwards, being connected together by cross-branches. In this first-formed portion of the colony there is no difficulty in distinguishing between Ascon-tubes and interspaces, the latter are wide, and there is no investing skin (pseudoderm) around the outer portion of the colony, and hence no definite pseudopores. But now as the colony grows older and larger a remarkable change in the mutual relations of the Ascon-tubes and interspaces takes place. This change affects only the newly formed portions of the colony, and leaves the old portion at the base in its original condition. The change takes place somewhat as follows:—As the young Ascon-tubes grow upwards the outer members of the colony fuse together so that their outer walls form a definite pseudoderm, leaving small apertures, the pseudopores, which still place the interspaces inside the colony in communication with the outside world. At the same time all the Ascon-tubes, outer and inner, increase in diameter and become extremely irregular in form, branching and anastomosing very freely. In proportion as the Ascon-tubes become expanded and irregular, so do the interspaces between them become constricted and well defined, until at last the tubes and interspaces appear to have changed places entirely, the tubes having become irregular interspaces, and the interspaces definite tubes. For this extraordinary condition I propose to use the term "reversal of the canal system." The pseudopores in the external skin of the colony now lead into narrow tubular inhalant canals, while the oscula on the top of the sponge communicate with the irregular spaces between these inhalant canals. These irregular spaces really represent the Ascon-tubes, and are lined on the *inside* of their walls by collared cells, while the narrow inhalant canals, which resemble in appearance the original Ascon-tubes, are lined on the *outside* of their walls by collared cells, so that a section across one of these inhalant canals looks like a section of an Ascon-tube turned inside out. The tubular oscula are also lined inside by collared cells. It is almost impossible to imagine a more complete loss of individuality on the part of the Ascon-persons which make up the colony than is exhibited in this sponge. It is difficult to convey in words a clear idea of the real state of the case, but I hope that reference to the figures will enable the reader to follow my description. Figure 1, Plate V., is a slightly diagrammatic view of a young colony cut in half vertically. Figure 2, Plate V., is a diagram, simplified as far as possible, and intended merely to show how the well-defined Ascon-tubes of the lower part of the colony become transformed into irregular interspaces in the upper portion, and *vice versâ*. The layer of collared cells is, as usual, coloured red. As already stated, this diagram is very much simplified; thus all the tubes are made vertical instead of branching and ramifying in every direction, and no inhalant canals are represented as entering from the sides of the colony as they mostly do in nature.

As, in the upward growth of the colony, the true Ascon-tubes gradually become transformed into irregular interspaces, and the true interspaces become gradually converted into definite tubes, a transition stage is reached at a certain point in which there are no definite tubes at all, and both Ascon-tubes and interspaces are represented by a series of irregular cavities. This condition usually prevails over a considerable portion of the centre of the colony (the portion marked x in Fig. 2, Pl. V.), so that here we have instead of tubes and interspaces two systems of irregular cavities. All the cavities of each system communicate freely with one another, but the one system never communicates with the other except through the minute inhalant pores (prosopyles) in the tube walls, which latter now form a very complex and irregular series of undulating membranes dividing the two systems of cavities. It is still possible to determine whether a given cavity in the sponge is gastral cavity or interspace by examining carefully its bounding membrane, and observing on which side the collared cells lie.* The undulating membrane (= Ascon-tube walls fused together) exhibits the usual characteristics of the Ascon-tube wall except for the presence in it of the yellow granules described above (p. 18). The mesoderm is, however, well developed, so that the wall averages about 0·035 mm. in thickness. I have not succeeded in detecting the prosopyles, apparently they are all closed.

Type D.—This type of canal system is exemplified in *Leucosolenia ventricosa*. In this species the colony forms large, compact, irregular masses, with uneven, undulating outer surface rising into mounds and ridges. In the typical

---

* As the collared cells very readily become detached and float away in spirit specimens, the task is rendered still more difficult, unless the material is very well preserved. If the collared cells have gone we can still tell on which side they lay by the position of other structures in the wall, as, for example, the position of the spicules and yellow granules. In well-preserved specimens, however, collared cells can easily be found.

forms there is in the centre of the colony a wide space or hollow in the form of a tube, penetrating almost to the base of the colony and opening above by a wide pseudosculum surrounded by a membranous frill or collar. This cavity is the pseudogaster. Its irregularity in form, the fact that it often shows subsidiary openings through the wall of the colony in addition to the terminal pseudosculum, and, above all, the fact that it is not lined by collared cells, all point to the conclusion that it is not a true gastral cavity but really lies outside the colony and is formed by the latter growing up in the form of a thick wall around a central space. Figure 8, Plate I, shows a very small specimen drawn three times the natural size. Figure 9, Plate I. shows the external appearance of a larger specimen, and Figure 10, Plate I. shows the same specimen cut in half longitudinally so as to exhibit the pseudogaster.

The colony (*i.e.* the thick wall of the pseudogaster) is made up of a dense plexus of branching and anastomosing Ascon-tubes separated from one another by well-developed interspaces and opening by true oscula into the pseudogaster.

All over the outer surface of the colony are numerous pseudopores, leading into the interspaces between the Ascon-tubes. They are small rounded or oval openings, ranging in diameter from about 0.3 to nearly 1 mm., and they are separated from one another by intervals of about the same breadth as themselves.

The investing skin or pseudoderm of the colony is in this species remarkably well developed and it is clearly differentiated into two parts. (1) The part covering the outside of the sponge and perforated by the pseudopores, and (2) The part lining the pseudogaster, not perforated (as a rule at any rate) by any pseudopores but by numerous true oscula, arranged in groups, as shown in Figure 10, Plate I.

Now the first of these two parts consists of a great number of Ascon-tubes fused together side by side so as to leave small but frequent interspaces, the pseudopores. These outer Ascon-tubes are much smaller than those in the interior of the colony, but their outer walls are very thick and strengthened by very large spicules. Hence the skin on the outer surface of the sponge is a thick *double* membrane in which the gastral cavities of its component Ascon-tubes are still present as small spaces lined by collared cells (Pl. IV., Fig. 4).

The portion of the pseudoderm which lines the pseudogaster constitutes, on the other hand, a very distinct and easily separable membrane, about 0·1 mm. in thickness, perforated by the exhalant openings of the Ascon-tubes (true oscula). This membrane, however, instead of showing a number of spaces lined by collared cells in the thickness between its two surfaces, is solid, consisting of the usual gelatinous mesodermal ground-substance with cells and spicules embedded in it, and lined *on each side* by ectoderm. The walls of the fused Ascon-tubes of which it is probably, like the outer portion of the pseudoderm, composed, have grown together and obliterated the gastral cavities, and the collared cells have disappeared. The openings of the Ascon-tubes (*i.e.*, oscula) appear to be formed secondarily; an Ascon-tube approaches the inner side of the membrane and the wall of the tube fuses with it. Then a perforation is established through the fused portion, leading from the gastral cavity of the Ascon-tube into the pseudogaster.

Around the pseudosculum the lining membrane of the pseudogaster is continued into a frill or collar (Pl. I., Fig. 10).

This is the only way in which I can explain the formation of the lining membrane of the pseudogaster, which differs essentially from the wall of an Ascontube in that it is not lined on either surface by collared cells, but on both by an epithelium of ordinary plate-like cells. We find an analogous process going on in the stalks of stipitate Calcisponges, which, originally formed out of one or more Ascontubes (or flagellated chambers in the higher forms), become solid by the obliteration of the cavities of the tubes and the disappearance of the collared cells.*

We come now to speak of the structure of the Ascon-tubes themselves. These, as already stated, are much narrower on the outside of the colony than elsewhere, and their outer walls are very thick (0.14 mm.) and contain numbers of very large spicules, so as to form a hard, resistent skin over the whole outer surface, penetrated by the pseudopores. As the Ascon-tubes approach the pseudogaster, towards which, notwithstanding their complex branching and anastomosing, the course of all the principal tubes is directed, their diameter increases and their walls become much thinner, so that while the Ascon-tubes themselves may have a diameter of 0.5 mm., their walls measure only about 0.05 mm. in thickness. Still these walls are very strong and firm, for they are supported by a very well developed skeleton of good-sized spicules, though much smaller than those on the outer surface.

The inhalant pores (prosopyles) in the walls of the Ascon-tubes are clearly visible in my preparations. They are simply circular apertures about 0·035 mm. in diameter.

The interspaces between the Ascon-tubes are wide and irregular, and continue right up to the lining membrane of the pseudogaster without diminishing in size. They communicate with the exterior through the small pseudopores on the outer surface of the colony.

Type E.—This very remarkable type of canal system, in which is shown the

---

* Compare my account of the development of the stalk in *Grantia labyrinthica*. (Studies on the Comparative Anatomy of Sponges III. Quarterly Journal of Microscopical Science, January, 1891.)

first indication of the subdivision of the gastral cavities of the Ascon-tubes by mesodermal ingrowths, is exemplified in *Leucosolenia proxima*.

The external appearance of this sponge is represented in Figures 1 and 2, Plate II. The colonies are small, only about 7 or 8 mm. in diameter, and attached to foreign objects, such as the stems of Algæ, by means of root-like processes. Over the upper surface of the colony are numerous small true oscula, each raised on a conical projection. The surface of the colony is pitted by numerous pseudopores. Except for the ingrowth of the mesoderm into the gastral cavities of the Ascon-tubes the canal system agrees with type B, as will be seen at once by reference to Figure 1, Plate VIII., representing a vertical section through the colony. The pseudopores on the outer surface of the colony are oval and measure about 0·27 mm. in longer diameter (in the specimen selected). They lead into perfectly irregular interspaces between the Ascon-tubes. The Ascon-tubes have thin walls measuring about 0·028 mm. in thickness. The inhalant pores (prosopyles) which perforate the tube-walls are, as usual, small circular apertures, easily visible in my preparations as areas devoid of collared cells and about 0·014 mm. in diameter; they may very likely be larger when fully opened. The Ascon-tubes of which the colony is composed collect together into several larger tubes, each of which leads up to and opens through an osculum.

In many of the Ascon-tubes, and especially in the larger branches which lead up to the oscula, there is plainly visible a network (Pl. VIII., Figs. 1, 2) of large, nucleated, stellate cells, sometimes appearing only near the wall of the tube, leaving the central portion of the gastral cavity quite empty, but at others stretching right across from wall to wall in the section. These stellate cells resemble ordinary mesodermal connective tissue cells except in their large size. The network which they form inside the gastral cavity remains connected with the mesoderm in the tube-wall by means of certain of the long slender processes of the cells, which penetrate between the collared cells of the endoderm. It appears to me highly probable that this network of cells has a nutritive function and serves to entangle food particles floating in the stream of water which flows through the tubes. There is no trace of a similar network in the interspaces between the Ascon-tubes.

It seems very strange that the mesoderm should thus break through the endoderm and come to lie on both sides of it. A somewhat analogous occurrence takes place in the case of the ovum of *Grantia labyrinthica*, which, as I have elsewhere[*] shown, breaks through the ectoderm and hangs suspended in the inhalant canals awaiting fertilisation;[†] but this is only a temporary condition and more easily understood, for the ovum at an early stage is known to possess the power of amœboid movement.

[*] "Studies on the Comparative Anatomy of Sponges, III. On the Anatomy of *Grantia labyrinthica*, Carter, and the so-called family Teichonidæ." Quarterly Journal of Microscopical Science, January, 1891.

[†] A careful re-examination of my preparations of *Grantia labyrinthica*, since this was written, has made me doubt the correctness of this observation, it being difficult to determine the true nature of the cavities in which the ova are suspended.

Type F.—This, the last type of reticulate canal system, is obviously a further development of type *E*, and hence especially interesting. It is best exemplified in *Leucosolenia wilsoni*. The canal system exactly resembles that of *Leucosolenia proxima* except that the mesodermal ingrowths into the gastral cavities of the Ascon-tubes are more strongly developed and the collared cells have spread in over them, so that the mesoderm is again covered all over by a layer of endoderm. The result of this proceeding is to divide the Ascon-tubes into a series of irregular and incomplete chambers, by means of what Hæckel terms "endogastric septa."

The entire sponge forms a low, irregular, encrusting growth (Pl. II., Figs. 3, 4) attached to the substratum by short, root-like processes. On the upper surface are the minute oscula, each on the summit of a small and almost solid, conical projection, and also numerous pseudopores which (on the upper surface of the sponge) are elongated and slit-like. Owing to the partial blocking up of the Ascon-tubes by the endogastric septa the whole sponge acquires an unusual degree of solidity, which is a very characteristic feature of the species.

The pseudopores lead direct into the irregular and perfectly empty interspaces, about which there is nothing to attract attention. These lead through the inhalant pores (prosopyles), which are easily visible in some parts of my preparations and measure about 0.02 mm. in diameter, into the Ascon-tubes. The Ascon-tubes, after collecting several together, open through the minute oscula at the apices of the conical projections (Pl. VII., Fig. 1). The appearance of the Ascon-tubes in section varies a good deal in different parts of the same colony and would seem to depend upon their age. In parts of the colony which seem to have been newly formed they are comparatively thin-walled, the wall of the tube being only about 0.04 mm. in thickness, while the inhalant pores (prosopyles) are clearly visible. The mesodermal ingrowths, also, are not nearly so strongly developed as in older tubes, consisting simply of a loose network of stellate cells, over which, however, the collared cells have already spread themselves. In the older parts of the colony the walls of the Ascon-tubes are thicker, the mesodermal ingrowths are more solid and the network of stellate cells of which they are at first composed is hardly visible through the dense layer of collared cells which invests it. This condition is represented in Figures 2 and 3, Plate VII. In the thick walls of the Ascon-tubes small stellate cells can be seen imbedded in the gelatinous ground-substance. The prosopyles are not visible in my sections of the older parts of the colony, being apparently closed.

No spicules are developed in the mesodermal ingrowths in the gastral cavities of the Ascon-tubes, so that if any doubt existed as to the position and extent of the originally simple and perfectly hollow Ascon-tubes the arrangement of the skeleton would be sufficient at once to determine it.

In many of the older tubes developing embryos* were found suspended in the middle of the gastral cavity, embedded in the mesoderm and surrounded by a peculiar capsule ; but these have already been described.

A similar, if not identical, condition of the Ascon-tubes, characterised by the formation of endogastric septa, was long since described by Hæckel in his *Ascetta primordialis* var. *loculosa* and *A. clathrus* var. *clathrina*.†

Section III. *RADIATA*.

This section of the genus, as its name implies, includes such species as exhibit a radiate structure—the sponge consisting of a single central Ascon-tube from which smaller tubes are budded off radially.

The only example of the section with which I am as yet acquainted is *Leucosolenia tripodifera*, a very interesting sponge originally described by Mr. Carter under the name *Clathrina tripodifera*. Fortunately, a considerable number of specimens of this sponge have come into my hands, including a piece of one of Mr. Carter's type specimens in the British Museum, so that I have been able fully to elucidate the anatomy of the species, an undertaking greatly facilitated by the large size to which the sponge grows. One specimen in my possession is nearly four inches (100 mm.) in height, and two inches (50 mm.) in diameter, it is represented of the natural size in Figure 6, Plate II. The remainder of my specimens, however, are none of them more than about one inch and a half (38 mm.) high, and three quarters of an inch (19 mm.) in diameter (Pl. II., Fig. 5).

The whole sponge resembles a very thick walled sack. The cavity of the sack is the gastral cavity of the central Ascon-tube, which is extraordinarily large, its transverse diameter being as great as, or greater than, the thickness of the wall of the sack. This cavity terminates in a wide osculum at the summit of the sponge (Pl. V., Fig. 3). The thick wall of the sack is made up of a great number of radial tubes given off from the central tube, into which they open by means of irregular groups of openings (Pl. V., Fig. 3). The way in which these radial tubes are formed is very plainly shown in one of my specimens, represented in a slightly diagrammatic manner in Figure 3, Plate V. At the summit of the sponge, immediately below the osculum, the wall of the large central Ascon-tube is very thin and membranous and there are no radial tubes developed as yet, so that it looks as if the osculum were surrounded by a membranous oscular fringe. The

---

* In the closely-allied species *Leucosolenia depressa*, ova only were found, in the same position as the embryos in *L. wilsoni*.

† "Die Kalkschwämme," Vol. 2, pp. 23, 35. Vol. 3, Pl. IV., Fig. 5.

uppermost part of the sponge, in fact, is still in the condition of a simple Ascon-person, with an unusually wide gastral cavity, whose thin walls (about 0·025 mm. thick) exhibit the usual structure, being lined by a layer of collared cells on the inside, and perforated by numerous inhalant pores (prosopyles).

At a short distance below the osculum, however, small, hollow buds make their appearance as outgrowths of the thin tube-wall. These buds are at first simple and unbranched. As they grow older they elongate and branch freely towards their distal ends, which terminate blindly; this condition prevails lower down in the colony. The branches of these numerous radial tubes lie close to one another, frequently touching, and form all together the thick wall of the sponge, which, of course, gradually increases in thickness as the colony grows older and is hence much thicker in the lower than in the upper portion of the sponge. Occasionally the cavities of the radial tubes communicate directly one with another but this does not seem to be at all general; an instance is shown in Figure 4, Plate V. As they branch towards their distal extremities the radial tubes become gradually narrower (Pl. V., Fig. 4) and their blind ends, for the most part in contact with one another, and protected by special spicules, form the outer surface of the sponge. Abundant small interstices are left between the ends of the radial tubes, which serve for the admission of water into the irregular interspaces between the radial tubes.

The structure of the individual radial tubes is shown in Figure 4, Plate V., and conforms to the usual Ascon type. The inhalant pores (prosopyles) are very distinctly shown in my preparations, they are simply circular apertures about 0.014 mm. in diameter.

The interspaces between the radial tubes are wide and irregular, widening as they approach the wall of the central Ascon-tube.

By cutting off portions of the wall of the central Ascon-tube and staining them separately, as well as by means of sections, I have been able to prove beyond doubt that the central cavity of the sponge is really lined by collared cells; its wall in fact presents the same structure as those of the radial tubes and is, like the latter, perforated by inhalant pores (prosopyles).

According to Mr. Carter this species is sometimes lipostomous, or devoid of osculum. He says,[*] describing the general form of the sponge, " conical, rather compressed, sessile, fixed, with cloaca and wide mouth; or ovoid and free, with cloacal cavity but *no* mouth, that is Haeckel's 'Auloplegma'-form." If Mr. Carter's account be correct it is a very remarkable thing, and I cannot at all understand how the stream of water is kept up through the sponge when there is no osculum.

[*]Annals and Magazine of Natural History, June, 1886, p. 505.

Certainly if the sponge is to continue to exist there must be some exhalant opening; moreover, if there be no osculum, why should there be a "cloacal cavity," as Mr. Carter calls it? I can understand the sponge having been perhaps damaged, and its growth consequently disturbed, and the osculum perhaps concealed by overgrowth of the neighbouring parts, but I cannot believe that there exists a sponge with no exhalant opening *(vide infrà)*.

Abnormalities in the form of the sponge may certainly occur, for in one of my specimens a kind of secondary osculum, if one may use the term, has been established near the base of the sponge, the radial tubes being absent over a small area and the thin wall of the central Ascon-tube perforated by a relatively large opening. Whether this is the result of injury or not it is impossible to say, but it seems not unlikely.

D.—THE CANAL SYSTEM OF THE CALCAREA HOMOCŒLA IN GENERAL.

After what has been said in the previous section there remains but little to add concerning the canal system of the Homocœla. The Victorian species of *Leucosolenia* so completely represent the genus that a knowledge of their anatomy is nearly all that is required to understand the anatomy of the Homocœla in general. The different forms of canal system enumerated and described above include with a few doubtful exceptions all the known types, and even add to those already described. The most important exceptions to this statement are what are known as the lipostomous forms, *i.e.*, forms without any osculum, including Haeckel's "artificial genera," *Clistolynthus* and *Auloplegma*, the former being a simple Olynthus with no osculum, and the latter a reticulate colony with no osculum. According to Haeckel the osculum may be entirely wanting, and then part of the prosopyles *(Tubi porales*, Haeckel) serve for the admission of water and part for its expulsion from the gastral cavity. It is a significant fact that amongst the numerous forms of Homocœla which I have had the opportunity of examining, I have never met with an example of what can be considered as true lipostomy. Certainly, as I have pointed out previously (in the case of *Leucosolenia lucasi* and *L. stolonifer)* the young Ascon-persons, formed as buds from the parent tube, at first end blindly and acquire an osculum only when they reach a certain age; but this is only an immature condition, and it seems to me not impossible that Haeckel's *Clistolynthus* may simply be an immature form in which the osculum is not yet developed. As to the *Auloplegma* form, I cannot help regarding this as simply a reticulate colony in which the oscula, opening either into a pseudogaster or directly on the surface of the colony, have been overlooked owing to their small size. In those forms provided with a pseudogaster which I have examined *(e.g., Leucosolenia ventricosa)* I have always been able to find direct communication between the gastral cavities of the Ascon-tubes and the pseudogaster. Then again we must not forget that in many sponges the osculum has the power of closing up entirely, and many forms described as lipostomous are probably only forms in which the osculum is temporarily closed, possibly by the action of the spirit in which the specimen has been preserved. I am unwilling to admit without further evidence that species exist in which the prosopyles serve both as incurrent and excurrent openings, there being no special excurrent opening or openings present in the adult sponge. Even, however, if we admit the existence of truly lipostomous *Homocœla*, there is no reason to alter or add to the classification of the canal system proposed above, for the lipostomous forms might stand side by side in the various groups with the ordinary osculate types.

Of the fifteen "artificial genera" described by Hæckel and diagnosed in the next section of the present memoir, the first seven, *Olynthus, Olynthella, Olynthium, Clistolynthus, Soleniscus, Solenula* and *Solenidium* fall under my section *Homocœla simplicia; Nardorus, Nardopsis, Nardoma, Tarrus, Tarropsis* and *Tarroma* are reticulate forms, while the last genus *Ascometra* is, according to Hæckel, a compound of several of the preceding genera in a single colony, but I prefer to regard it as a colony composed of individuals in various stages of development.

Concerning the types of canal system represented by von Lendenfeld's genera *Homoderma* and *Leucopsis*[*] there is little to say; *Homoderma*, if it really be a Homocœlous sponge, comes under my section *Radiata*, while *Leucopsis* is too imperfectly described to be taken into serious consideration, though as far as we can judge from the description and figure it appears to be simply a reticulate *Leucosolenia* with well developed pseudogaster.

As to Hæckel's *Ascaltis canariensis* and *Ascaltis lamarckii*, which von Lendenfeld now[†] includes in his family *Homodermidæ*, I cannot see any reason for placing them amongst the radiate *Homocœla*. The endodermal papillæ which project into the gastral cavity around the apical rays of the quadriradiates appear, to judge from Hæckel's description and figures,[‡] to be merely exaggerations of the slight projections of the endoderm which frequently surround the bases of projecting spicule-rays (*cf. Leucosolenia stolonifer*, Pl. VI., Fig. 1) and they certainly in no way indicate the formation of radial tubes, which originate as outgrowths and not as ingrowths. A moment's reflection will show that such ingrowths of the endoderm as those figured by Hæckel could never give rise to the formation of radial tubes.

[*] Proceedings of the Linnean Society of New South Wales. Vol. IX., Part 4, pp. 1088, 1089.
[†] "Das System der Spongien." (Separatabdruck aus den Abhandlungen der Senckenbergischen naturforschenden Gesellschaft.) Frankfurt a.M. 1890.
[‡] "Die Kalkschwämme," Vol. 2, pp. 52, 60. Vol. 3, Plate IX, Figs. 1, 2, 3, 5.

III.—THE CLASSIFICATION OF THE CALCAREA HOMOCŒLA.

In classifying the Calcarea we have two primary sets of characters to guide us; these are (1) the structure of the individual (person) and (2) the structure of the sponge-colony as a whole.

Hæckel apparently considers the structure of the individual to be the most important. In his great monograph of the group, he distinguishes three "families" of calcareous sponges :—

1. *Ascones*,* = Calcisponges " mit Loch-Canälen."
2. *Leucones*, = Calcisponges " mit Ast-Canälen."
3. *Sycones*, = Calcisponges " mit Strahl-Canälen."

But here already we are landed in confusion, for the " Loch-Canälen," " Ast-Canälen," and " Strahl-Canälen " are not homologous or even comparable structures. The Loch-Canälen of the Ascones (Homocœla) are simply the inhalant pores (prosopyles) in the thin wall of the Ascon-person, while the " Strahl-Canälen" of the Sycones are totally distinct structures, being really, according to Hæckel, the homologues of entire Ascon-persons, and the Sycon-person as a whole equivalent to a colony of Ascon-persons formed by gemmation. Each " Strahl-Canal " is, according to this view,† nothing but an Ascon-person, and each certainly has its own " Loch-Canälen" exactly as in a typical Homocœlous (Ascon) form.

If Hæckel's opinion that the Sycon-person is equivalent to a colony of Ascon-persons is correct, he really makes use of the form of the colony and not of the structure of the individual as the family characteristic of the Sycones. When, however, he comes to subdivide the Ascones (= Homocœla) into genera he denies the value of the form of the colony as a whole as a natural character, relying entirely for the distinction of what he terms his " natural" genera upon the structure of the skeleton, and using the form of the colony only in what he terms his " artificial " system.

Accordingly we find two schemes of classification in Hæckel's monograph placed side by side, the artificial and natural, as he calls them. We will consider at present

---
* Hæckel's *Ascones* are equivalent to our *Homocœla*, his *Leucones* and *Sycones* to the *Heterocœla*.

† I do not wish to commit myself at present to any definite view on this question, which will be discussed in a later portion of the present work.

only that part of each system which deals with the Calcarea Homocœla (Ascones), of which the following is an epitome* :—

(A.) NATURAL SYSTEM.

Family *Ascones*.

Genus 1. *Ascetta.*—Spicules all triradiate.
Genus 2. *Ascilla.*—Spicules all quadriradiate.
Genus 3. *Ascyssa.*—Spicules all oxeote.
Genus 4. *Ascaltis.*—Spicules partly triradiate, partly quadriradiate.
Genus 5. *Ascortis.*—Spicules partly triradiate, partly oxeote.
Genus 6. *Asculmis.*—Spicules partly quadriradiate, partly oxeote.
Genus 7. *Ascandra.*—Spicules partly triradiate, partly quadriradiate and partly oxeote.

(B.) ARTIFICIAL SYSTEM.

Family 1. *Olynthida*.

Ascones consisting of a single person with a single osculum.

Genus 1. *Olynthus.*—A single person with naked osculum.
Genus 2. *Olynthella.*—A single person with probosciform osculum.
Genus 3. *Olynthium.*—A single person with the osculum provided with a fringe.

Family 2. *Clystolinthida*.

Ascones consisting of a single person without any osculum.

Genus 4. *Clystolynthus.*—A single person without an osculum.

Family 3. *Soleniscida*.

Ascones consisting of a colony of simple persons provided with oscula.

Genus 5. *Soleniscus.*—A colony of simple persons with naked oscula.
Genus 6. *Solenula.*—A colony of simple persons with probosciform oscula.
Genus 7. *Solenidium.*—A colony of simple persons with fringed oscula.

* " Die Kalkschwämme," Vol. I., pp. 84, 85.

Family 4. *Nardopsida.*

Ascones forming a colony with a single common osculum.

Genus 8. *Nardorus.*—A colony with a single naked osculum.
Genus 9. *Nardopsis.*—A colony with a single probosciform osculum.
Genus 10. *Nardoma.*—A colony with a single fringed osculum.

Family 5. *Tarromida.*

Ascones in which the sponge is composed of several colonies, each with a single osculum.

Genus 11. *Tarrus.*—A colony composed of several *Nardorus* colonies.
Genus 12. *Tarropsis.*—A colony composed of several *Nardopsis* colonies.
Genus 13. *Tarroma.*—A colony composed of several *Nardoma* colonies.

Family 6. *Auloplegmida.*

Ascones consisting of a colony with no osculum.

Genus 14. *Auloplegma.*—A colony with no osculum.

Family 7. *Ascometrida.*

Ascones consisting of a colony in which several generic forms are united.

Genus 15. *Ascometra.*—A colony consisting of several generic forms united.

The second of these two extremely ingenious schemes of classification is well termed by its author artificial, but this term, as it seems to me, applies equally well to the so-called "natural" system. Neither system is in itself sufficient, and the use of the two side by side by Hæckel has led to an almost hopeless confusion in the nomenclature of genera and species, as every spongologist finds to his cost when endeavouring to identify a calcareous sponge.

The fault of each system lies in the fact that it is based upon a single group of characters, and the inadequateness of the "natural system," which Hæckel principally uses, is shown by the host of "generic," "specific," and "connective" varieties which he has been obliged to create. The first species described in Hæckel's monograph is *Ascetta primordialis* and this embraces seven generic varieties, four specific varities and three connective varieties, each with a different name. The only "Species-character" given is a short description of the spicules, and no type of the species is described; and so on for the other species.

All forms of Homocœla, no matter what their anatomical peculiarities, which happen to have spicules of the same shape, are brought by Hæckel under a single "species." Now there are only three fundamental forms of spicules in the entire group of calcareous sponges, viz., the triradiate, quadriradiate and oxeote, and each of these may vary greatly in shape within a single specimen. Moreover some portions of a colony may contain say oxeote or quadriradiate spicules, while other portions taken from the same specimen may contain none. Hæckel was well aware of this variation in the spiculation and hence his "connective varieties," which often bring the same species under two or three distinct genera.

I grant that there are certain forms of spicules which may be regarded as typical for each species, but the presence of similar spicules is not alone sufficient to justify us in including under one specific name forms which otherwise differ widely in organisation.

Hæckel's natural genera are particularly artificial, and this might be expected when we see that the same series of generic diagnoses, depending solely upon the combinations of the three types of spicules, is made to serve for all his three families of calcareous sponges.

Since neither of Hæckel's alternative systems will satisfy the requirements of the modern zoologist we must find a new method, and in this new method we must be content to follow the example of workers in other branches of zoology and give up all hope of finding a royal road to classification. In other words, we must make use of as many characters as possible and not of as few, and in this way—*classifying by an assemblage of characters*[*]—we may fairly hope to make satisfactory progress. At the same time we must not forget that Hæckel's classification of the Calcarea was the first serious attempt at anything of the kind; that he had an extremely difficult task to deal with, and that immense credit is due to him for the energy and perseverance with which he led the way in this department of biology. All schemes of classification are but tentative and each must give place to later modifications as our knowledge advances, for evolution plays as important a part in our study of organisms as it does in the history of the organisms themselves.

Of course we shall find that different characters often contradict one another, forms which agree in spiculation may differ widely in canal-system, and *vice-versâ*. So great is the variation in both these characters amongst the Calcarea Homocœla and so difficult is it to determine which is the most important that Poléjaeff has, in his work on the Calcarea of the "Challenger" Expedition, abandoned all Hæckel's seven natural genera of Homocœla and fallen back upon the old genus *Leucosolenia*

---

[*] "No doubt organic beings, like all other objects, can be classed in many ways, either artificially by single characters or more naturally by a number of characters."—Darwin, "Origin of Species," Ed. VI., p. 364.

of Bowerbank as the sole genus of the group. In this I agree with Poléjaeff, but at the same time, as a mere matter of convenience and not necessarily as indicating genetic relationship, I prefer to subdivide the genus into sections and subsections according to the nature of the canal system of the colony. I prefer to make use of the canal system for this purpose rather than the spiculation, for I have frequently found the spiculation varying greatly in different parts of the same colony but never so the canal system (except in cases where a later-formed portion of the colony shows an advance in organisation as compared with an earlier-formed portion, as, for example, in *Leucosolenia cavata*; but this is simply a case of different ontogenetic stages being present simultaneously. May not a similar state of affairs have given rise to Miklucho-Macleay's* and Hæckel's statements as to the co-existence of different types of canal system in the same colony, as in Hæckel's genus *Ascometra?*). On the other hand I have excellent series of specimens of obviously the same species in which the canal system is remarkably constant (*e.g., Leucosolenia cavata, L. tripodifera, L. pelliculata*). Moreover the canal system offers a wider range of characters to choose from than do the combinations of spicules, of which seven only are possible.

The classification which I therefore propose to make use of for the Calcarea Homocœla is as follows :—

Order Homocœla (Poléjaeff).

Calcareous sponges in which the endoderm consists throughout of collared cells.

Genus, *Leucosolenia* (Bowerbank).

With the characters of the order.

Section 1. *Homocœla Simplicia*.

Homocœla in which the Ascon-persons either remain solitary and do not form colonies or they form simple colonies in which the component Ascon-persons may branch but never form complex anastomoses nor give off radial tubes, so that the individuality of the different members of the colony is easily recognisable.

Section 2. *Homocœla Reticulata.*†

Homocœla in which the sponge-colony forms a more or less complex network of branching and anastomosing tubes, so that it is no longer possible to distinguish the individual Ascon-persons of which the colony is composed.

---

* Jenaische Zeitschrift, Vol. IV., 1868.
† This section is practically synonymous with Gray's genus *Clathrina*, used by Carter in his descriptions of the Victorian sponges (*loc. cit.*).

Subsection 1. *Indivisa.*

The gastral cavities of the Ascon-tubes composing the colony retain their primitive hollow condition, there being no ingrowths of mesoderm or endoderm.

Subsection 2. *Subdivisa.*

The gastral cavities of the Ascon-tubes are more or less completely subdivided into chambers by ingrowths of mesoderm or of both mesoderm and endoderm.

SECTION 3. *Homocœla Radiata.*

Homocœla in which the sponge consists of a single, central Ascon-tube from which secondary tubes are budded off radially.

This classification will, so far as I am aware, serve to include all the known forms of Homocœla with the doubtful exceptions of Hæckel's *Ascometra* and von Lendenfeld's *Leucopsis*,* concerning both of which we require further details. *Ascometra* may, as I have already suggested, simply represent a series of ontogenetic stages present at the same time, for there can be little doubt that the most complex adult forms pass through several stages, beginning with the Olynthus, in their life history; while the extremely doubtful *Leucopsis* is probably only one of the *Homocœla reticulata*, and whatever it is it is so insufficiently described that we cannot possibly recognise it.

In distinguishing species all characters are of use, and a well-marked difference in any one character is, in my opinion, a sufficient justification for a distinct specific name. This, of course, necessitates a good many specific names, but it is better to have too many than too few, and so long as each form is properly described increase of species only adds to our knowledge, while the merging of many forms under one name makes hopeless confusion, for the author who does so seldom thinks it necessary to give an adequate description of each variety and it then becomes impossible to sort them out and to determine which is really the type of the species.

The term species is, as I understand it, a purely arbitrary one, meaning simply an assemblage of individuals more or less resembling one another and presumably descended from a common parent, but whether a particular individual belongs to a particular species or not is a question which each observer must decide for himself.†

---

* Proceedings of the Linnean Society of New South Wales, Vol. IX., part 4, p. 1080.

† "From these remarks it will be seen that I look at the term species as one arbitrarily given, for the sake of convenience, to a set of individuals closely resembling each other, and that it does not essentially differ from the term variety, which is given to less distinct and more fluctuating forms. The term variety, again, in comparison with mere individual differences, is also applied arbitrarily, for convenience' sake."—Darwin, "Origin of Species," Ed. VI., p. 42.

IV.—DESCRIPTIONS OF THE VICTORIAN SPECIES OF CALCAREA HOMOCŒLA.

I follow Poléjaeff[*] in dividing the calcareous sponges into two orders, *Homocœla* and *Heterocœla*. The term Homocœla, as already stated, is synonymous with Haeckel's term *Ascones* and the diagnosis of the order is the same as that of the sole genus (*Leucosolenia*) comprised therein.

Genus *Leucosolenia*, Bowerbank.[†]

Diagnosis.—Calcareous sponges in which the endoderm consists throughout of collared cells.

In the following arrangement of the Victorian species of *Leucosolenia* I include only such as I have been able to examine myself or such as are sufficiently fully described as to make their indentity tolerably certain. I give at the end a list, together with the original descriptions, of what must at present be considered as doubtful species stated to have been found in Victorian seas.

Section 1. *Simplicia*.

The Ascon-persons either remain solitary and do not form colonies, or they form simple colonies in which the component Ascon-persons may branch but never form complex anastomoses nor give off radial tubes, so that the individuality of the different members of the colony is easily recognisable.

1. *Leucosolenia lucasi*, n. sp.

(Pl. I., Fig. 1; Pl. IV., Fig. 1; Pl. IX., Fig. 1.)

(*a.*) *General Appearance and Canal System.*—The sponge (Pl. I., Fig. 1) forms loose colonies, the Ascon-persons being connected at their bases by a hollow spongorhiza which creeps over foreign objects. The Ascon-persons are small, cylindrical, thin-walled tubes, 2 or 3 mm. in height and about 0·7 mm. in diameter. When fully grown there is a wide osculum at the summit of each individual. The outer surface of the tubes is very minutely hispid and the colour in spirit is white.

---

[*] Report on the Calcarea of the "Challenger" Expedition, p. 22.
[†] Philosophical Transactions of the Royal Society of London, 1862, p. 1091.

Particulars of the canal system are given on pp. 24, 25.

(b.) *Arrangement of the Skeleton.*—The skeleton consists of quadriradiate, triradiate and oxeote spicules. The quadriradiates and triradiates are arranged in a single layer in the thickness of the mesoderm, the apical rays of the quadriradiates projecting into the gastral cavity. The oxeotes have their broader ends embedded in the mesoderm, while their narrow ends project outwards and upwards through the ectoderm and give to the outer surfaces of the tubes their hispid appearance. The arrangement of the spicules is shown in Fig. 1, Pl. IV.

(c.) *The Spicules.* (Pl. IX., Fig. 1).

(1.) *Triradiates.*—These are sagittal, but the three angles are about equal. The basal ray is long and gradually sharp-pointed, measuring 0·1 mm. in length by 0·005 mm. in diameter at the base. The oral rays are slightly curved away from one another, gradually sharp-pointed, 0.07 mm. long.

(2.) *Quadriradiates.*—These are of about the same size and shape as the triradiates with the addition of the apical ray, which is shorter than the others, gradually sharp-pointed, curving slightly upwards and projecting freely into the gastral cavity.

(3.) *Oxeotes.*—These are irregularly fusiform, sharply pointed at both ends but broader at one end than at the other; usually bent suddenly at a slight angle near the broader end; often slightly and irregularly curved; tapering gradually to a fine point at the narrow end but with a very slight annular swelling at a short distance below the apex. They measure up to 0·16 mm. in length by 0·005 mm. in diameter at the broadest part.

(d.) *Affinities.*—In external appearance this species resembles Haeckel's *Soleniscus variabilis** but it differs markedly in the form of the spicules.

(e.) *Locality.*—Outside Port Phillip Heads. (Coll. J. B. Wilson.)

2. *Leucosolenia stolonifer*, n. sp.

(Pl. I., Fig. 2; Pl. VI., Figs. 1, 2, 3; Pl. IX., Fig. 2.)

(a.) *General Appearance and Canal System.*—The sponge (Pl. I., Fig. 2) consists of a colony of Ascon-persons springing vertically from a slender, tubular

---

* "Die Kalkschwämme," Vol. III., Pl. 19, Fig. 6.

spongorhiza which spreads horizontally in every direction over the substratum on which the colony is growing. Occasionally, but only rarely, the Ascon-persons anastomose with one another. The spongorhiza also produces short downward outgrowths whereby the colony is attached to the substratum. The Ascon-persons are cylindrical tubes much wider than the spongorhiza, each provided, when adult, with a terminal osculum. They attain a height of about 35 mm. and a diameter of about 3·5 mm., narrowing slightly towards the osculum. The wall of the tube is about 0·14 mm. thick and distinctly hispid on its outer surface. The colour in spirit is white.

Particulars of the canal system are given on pp. 25, 26.

(*b.*) *Arrangement of the Skeleton.*—The skeleton consists of quadriradiate and oxeote spicules. The quadriradiates are very closely packed in the mesoderm, forming a rather confused layer, with their facial rays freely overlapping and their apical rays projecting into the gastral cavity. The oxeotes have their broader ends embedded in the mesoderm and their narrow ends projecting outwards and obliquely upwards through the ectoderm and giving to the surface of the tube its hispid character.

(*c.*) *The Spicules* (Pl. IX., Fig. 2).

(1.) *Quadriradiates.*—These vary a good deal both in size and form. They are generally more or less markedly sagittal but not very strongly so, and may be almost or quite regular. The rays may be all straight or the oral rays may be slightly curved. The apical ray is usually short, slender, sharp-pointed, and curved towards the oral angle; much shorter and slenderer than the facial rays; in a small, but by no means insignificant proportion of the spicules, however, it becomes enormously exaggerated, measuring as much as 0·6 mm. in length and 0·035 mm. in diameter at the base, so that its dimensions greatly exceed those of the facial rays; when developed in this way it is often irregularly bent. The facial rays are usually conical, gradually sharp-pointed, and measure about 0·2 by 0·015 mm.; sometimes they are slightly constricted at the base.

(2.) *Oxeotes.*—These are large, asymmetrically fusiform spicules, the widest part being much nearer to one end than to the other. They may be quite straight but are more generally somewhat curved like a sickle, the curvature may be even or more or less irregular. They are sharply pointed at each end. When fully developed they measure about 0·7 by 0·03 mm.

The variability and frequent irregularity of the spicules in this species render them difficult to describe accurately, but it is hoped that the figures will serve to give a correct idea of them.

(d.) *Affinities.*—In external form this species bears a marked resemblance to Hæckel's *Ascometra variabilis** while in spiculation it approaches the *Asculmis* form of the same species.† Hæckel's species, however, differs from *Leucosolenia stolonifer* in the presence of an annular swelling near one extremity of the oxeote spicule and in the wavy curvature of the rays of the quadriradiates, moreover triradiate spicules are almost always present. Carter's *Aphroceras asconoides*, from near Port Phillip Heads, perhaps makes a nearer approach to our species and I at first believed the two to be identical. In *Leucosolenia asconoides*, however, judging from Carter's description‡ the oxeote spicules are much larger and symmetrically fusiform, while the quadriradiates have much slenderer rays and none of them appear to have the greatly enlarged apical ray characteristic of *Leucosolenia stolonifer*. I have five distinct colonies of this species and in all five the enlarged apical rays projecting into the gastral cavity form a conspicuous feature.

(e.) *Locality.*—Near Port Phillip Heads. (Coll. J. B. Wilson.)

3. *Leucosolenia asconoides*, Carter, sp.

Aphroceras asconoides, Carter, Annals and Magazine of Natural History, August 1886, p. 134.

(As I have not had the opportunity of examining this species myself I must rely entirely on Mr. Carter's description, which, in conjunction with the manuscript illustrations of the species which he has kindly sent me, appears to me to be sufficiently detailed for recognition.)

(a.) *General Appearance and Canal System.*—The sponge consists of a colony of Ascon-persons growing from a contracted base. The individuals are long, narrow, tubular, sessile, somewhat compressed, diminishing in size towards the free end, which is truncate, and contracted towards the other, which is fixed. They attain a height of about 37 mm. and a diameter of nearly 3 mm. They often branch slightly. The osculum, at the upper end of the tube, is not surrounded by any fringe. In dry specimens the outer surface is even, glistening, composed of a layer

---

* "Die Kalkschwämme," Vol. III., Pl. 18, Fig. 9.
† *Op. cit.* Vol. II., p. 108; Vol. III., Pl. 16, Fig. 4.
‡ Annals and Magazine of Natural History, August, 1886, p. 134.

of very large oxeote spicules arranged longitudinally and very near together, between which are the inhalant pores. The wall of the tube is 0·2 mm. in thickness. The colour (dry or in spirit ?) is yellowish white.

(*b.*) *Arrangement of the Skeleton.*—The skeleton consists of quadriradiate and oxeote spicules, arranged in the normal manner, the quadriradiates forming an internal layer with the apical rays projecting into the gastral cavity and the oxea forming an external layer. Judging from the description the oxea do not project beyond the outer surface of the tube but the surface is minutely hispid from the projection of some of the facial rays of the quadriradiates.

(*c.*) *The Spicules.*

(1) *Quadriradiates.*—These are comparatively small and delicate spicules, with very slender rays. They are more or less sagittal in form, with a long basal ray and two very much shorter oral rays extended almost at right angles to the basal ray. The basal ray is perfectly straight and tapers gradually to a fine point. The oral rays are also finely and gradually pointed, but curve slightly backwards towards the apex of the basal ray. The basal ray measures about 0·375 by 0·004 mm. and the oral rays about 0·18 by 0·004 mm.

(2.) *Oxeotes.*—These are very long and stout, symmetrically fusiform, slightly curved and gradually sharp-pointed at each end, averaging about 2·0 mm. in length by 0·1 mm. in diameter.

(*d.*) *Affinities.*—Although Mr. Carter places this species amongst the Leucons, yet his description makes it perfectly clear that it is really one of the *Homocœla simplicia* and nearly related to *Leucosolenia stolonifer*. If the description be correct, however, as there is no reason to doubt it is, it is readily distinguishable from that species by the size and shape of the spicules, and possibly also by the external form, for there appears to be no spongorhiza and the individuals are stated to grow from a contracted base. (*Vide* also the remarks on the affinities of *Leucosolenia stolonifer, suprà.*)

(*e.*) *Locality.*—Near Port Phillip Heads. (Coll. J. B. Wilson.)

Section 2. *Reticulata.*

The sponge-colony forms a more or less complex network of branching and anastomosing tubes, and it is no longer possible to distinguish the individual Ascon-persons of which the colony is composed.

Subsection 1. *Indivisa.*

The gastral cavities of the Ascon-tubes composing the colony retain the primitive hollow condition, there being no ingrowth of the mesoderm or endoderm.

4. *Leucosolenia dubia*, n. sp.

(Pl. I., Fig. 3 ; Pl. IX., Fig. 3.)

(*a.*) *General Appearance and Canal System.*—The sponge-colony forms irregular, low-growing masses, composed of a network of branching and anastomosing, more or less cylindrical Ascon-tubes. The size of the interspaces between the tubes varies greatly in different specimens and, indeed, in different parts of the same specimen. No definite external skin (pseudoderm) is formed, the interspaces between the surface tubes being as wide as in the interior of the colony. In compact colonies the surface has a curious vermiculated appearance, in loose ones (Pl. I., Fig. 3) it is a lattice-work with oval or rounded meshes. On the under surface of the colony are sometimes present little root-like processes, which serve for attachment. The oscula, when discoverable, are visible as very small, round apertures, situate on the apices of small papillæ formed by the anastomosis of several Ascon-tubes.

The diameter of the cylindrical Ascon-tubes varies a good deal in different parts of the same colony, say from 0.5 to 1 mm. To the naked eye some of the tubes appear smooth on the outer surface, others minutely but distinctly hispid. The colour in spirit is white or nearly so. Further details as to the canal system, which conforms to type A, will be found on p. 28.

(*b.*) *Arrangement of the Skeleton.*—The skeleton consists of triradiate and oxeote spicules. The former are arranged in a confused layer in the mesoderm, the spicules being placed close together with rays overlapping. The latter occur only in certain parts of the colony, namely, in some, and apparently only some, of the outer Ascon-tubes. Hence a boiled out preparation from one part of a specimen may show no oxeote spicules at all, while another from a different part of the same specimen contains plenty of them. When present the oxeotes project more or less from the outer surface of the Ascon-tubes, whence the hispid appearance of the latter.

(*c.*) *The Spicules* (Pl. IX., Fig. 3.)

(1.) *Triradiates.*—These are approximately regular or slightly sagittal. The rays are fairly stout, conical or subfusiform in shape, fairly sharply but rather abruptly pointed, often a little irregular in diameter and mode of pointing ; measuring about 0·18 by 0·014 mm.

(2.) *Oxeotes.*—These are stout, club-shaped, often irregularly and strongly curved, very broad near one end and tapering gradually to a fine point at the other; abruptly but sharply pointed at the broad end. The size of these spicules is very variable, up to 0·43 by 0·02 mm.

In addition to the spicules above-mentioned I have met with a few quadriradiates, which do not seem, however, to be characteristic but only occasional.

(d.) *Affinities.*—There are probably several distinct species which closely resemble *Leucosolenia dubia* in general form and canal system, as, for example, certain forms of Hæckel's *Ascetta coriacea* and *A. clathrus*, which differ from it, however, in spiculation. In one character *Leucosolenia dubia* strikingly resembles *L. cavata*, to be described later on, namely, in the presence of great numbers of "yellow granules" embedded in the mesoderm. The structure and meaning of these bodies has already been discussed. They appear to be of constant occurrence in the species in which they are found and remind one in this respect of the curious dumb-bell-shaped filaments, also of unknown significance, present in the *Hircinidæ* amongst horny sponges. Indeed, it is by no means improbable that the specimens which I distinguish as *Leucosolenia dubia* may be young forms of *L. cavata*, for the general organisation (including spiculation) resembles closely that of the first-formed part of a colony of *L. cavata*. *L. dubia*, however, attains a considerable size (the largest specimen being about 62 mm. in greatest breadth and 20 mm. thick) without acquiring the very peculiar canal system of *L. cavata*.

(e.) *Locality.*—Near Port Phillip Heads. (Coll. J. B. Wilson.)

5. *Leucosolenia stipitata*, n. sp.

(Pl. I., Figs. 4, 5, 6; Pl. IV., Fig. 2; Pl. IX., Fig. 5.)

(a.) *General Appearance and Canal System.*—This is a very minute sponge, consisting of a more or less oval body perched on the summit of a short, slender stem attached at its lower extremity to some foreign body. The total height of the sponge is only about 12 mm. Figures 4 and 5, Plate I., show two specimens of the natural size, and Figure 6, Plate I., one of them greatly enlarged. The stem is solid and cylindrical. The body has the reticulate surface characteristic of this section of the genus, the pseudopores being rather large in proportion to the size of the sponge. On the summit of the body is a relatively large osculum. Only one osculum is present in the specimens figured, but I should imagine that there might sometimes be more in older specimens. The colour in spirit is white.

The canal system conforms to type B., and is described on p. 28 and illustrated in Figure 2, Plate IV.

(b.) *Arrangement of the Skeleton.*—The skeleton consists of triradiate spicules only, arranged in a single layer in the mesoderm. In the outer skin (pseudoderm) the spicules are arranged fairly regularly, in a single layer, with all the basal rays pointing towards the stem. In the stem the spicules are very densely and rather irregularly arranged, but still with a large proportion of the basal rays pointing downwards.

(c.) *The Spicules* (Pl. IX., Fig. 5).—As already stated these are all triradiate; they are more or less sagittal, and the rays are all straight, conical or subfusiform, and gradually sharp-pointed. In the spicules of the pseudoderm the basal ray measures up to 0·1 by 0·01 mm., and the lateral rays about 0·07 by 0·0085 mm. The spicules of the deeper parts of the body are more nearly regular and somewhat slenderer than those at the surface. The rays of the dermal spicules are slightly curved, in such a manner that the centre of the spicule is uplifted above the plane in which the apices of the three rays lie.

(d.) *Affinities.*—This species very closely resembles von Lendenfeld's *Ascetta macleayi*[*] in external form and spiculation; indeed for a long time I regarded the two as identical, but if von Lendenfeld's description of the canal system in *Leucosolenia macleayi* be correct the two species differ very markedly in this respect. According to von Lendenfeld *Ascetta macleayi* is one of Hæckel's "Anloplegma" forms, with a pseudogaster and pseudosculum, while in *Leucosolenia stipitata* there is no pseudogaster and the osculum is a true osculum. It appears to me very desirable to distinguish by different names forms which differ so widely in anatomical characters, but this question has been already discussed in the section of the present work dealing with classification.

The species closely resembles one form of Miklucho-Maclear's *Guancha blanca*,[†] but considering the great variety of forms included under that name and the fact that the spicules appear to be much stouter and more sharply pointed in *Leucosolenia stipitata* it seems best to give a distinct name to the latter.

(e.) *Locality.*—Near Port Phillip Heads. (Coll. J. B. Wilson.)

6. *Leucosolenia pulcherrima*, n. sp.

(Pl. I., Fig. 7 ; Pl. IV., Fig. 3 ; Pl. X., Fig.3.)

(a.) *General Appearance and Canal System.*—The sponge consists of a relatively large body perched on the end of a short stalk. Figure 7, Plate I., represents a typical example multiplied seven diameters. The body is irregularly ovoid in shape,

---

[*] Proceedings of the Linnean Society of New South Wales, Vol. IX., Part 4, p. 1086.
[†] Jenaische Zeitschrift, Band IV., 1868.

compressed laterally, and with a somewhat flattened upper surface on which are several true oscula each surrounded by a membranous oscular fringe. The sides of the body exhibit a number of narrow ridges, of which the principal ones run vertically, branching and anastomosing more or less and connected by less pronounced, more or less transverse ridges; between the ridges are numerous interspaces of irregularly rounded shape, these are the pseudopores. The height of the whole colony is only about 10 mm. and the greatest breadth about 6 mm. (in the specimen figured). In some specimens the ridges are much less regularly arranged, and the oscular fringes not so well developed. The ridges are, of course, the outer surfaces of the outer Ascon-tubes of the colony. The colour in spirit is white.

The canal system conforms to type B (described on p. 28) and is illustrated in Figure 3, Plate IV.

(b.) *Arrangement of the Skeleton.*—The skeleton consists of triradiate spicules only, arranged in the usual manner. In the outer Ascon-tubes the spicules are often sagittal and the basal ray then points downward as usual.

(c.) *The Spicules* (Pl. X., Fig. 3).—The triradiate spicules vary considerably in form according to their position in the sponge, so that we may roughly distinguish between deep and dermal spicules. The dermal spicules are sometimes nearly equiangular and equiradiate, but with the rays strongly curved so that the centre of the spicule is uplifted considerably above the level of the plane in which the apices of the three rays lie. The rays are stout, conical and not very sharply pointed, measuring about 0·056 by 0·008 mm. Very frequently, however, the dermal spicules become markedly sagittal, the lateral (or oral) rays embracing a much wider angle (nearly 180° in some cases) and curving somewhat towards one another, while the basal ray may be elongated to about 0·1 mm. The deep spicules, lying in the walls of the internal Ascon-tubes, are approximately equiangular and equiradiate, with the rays lying pretty much in one plane, so that the spicule would lie almost or quite flat on a plane surface. The rays are straight and slender, of nearly the same diameter all along until close to the apex and then rather abruptly and not very sharply pointed. They measure about 0·084 mm. in length by 0·0042 mm. in diameter.

(d.) *Affinities.*—This species is obviously closely related to *L. stipitata* and I should not be at all surprised to find a perfect series of intermediate forms. Typical examples of each are, however, easily distinguishable by their external appearance, and they may conveniently receive separate names.

(e.) *Locality.*—Near Port Phillip Heads. (Coll. J. B. Wilson.)

7. *Leucosolenia pelliculata*, n. sp.

(Pl. III., Fig. 2; Pl. VIII., Fig. 7; Pl. X., Figs. 1, 2.)

(*a.*) *General Appearance and Canal System.*—The sponge forms rather small, low-growing, lobular masses of irregular shape (Pl. III., Fig. 2,) and with a very well marked outer skin or pseudoderm. The largest specimen in the collection is scarcely 37 mm. in greatest diameter. The skin is smooth and somewhat glabrous. Here and there over the surface of the lobes are scattered small, true oscula, generally surrounded by a very slightly developed oscular fringe. The general external appearance of the sponge varies a good deal on account of the variation in the size of the pseudopores. In some specimens these are very minute and very closely arranged, so small that to the naked eye the surface has merely a minutely punctate appearance, while in others they are a little over 0·5 mm. in diameter. Even in different parts of the same specimen they vary much in size. The small size of the pseudopores causes the skin to appear unusually well developed, whence the specific name *pelliculata*.

The colour of the sponge in spirit may be pure white, pale brown or even pinkish.* The canal system belongs to type B and agrees precisely with that of *Leucosolenia pulcherrima*, figured on Plate IV., Figure 3. The walls of the Ascon-tubes are characteristically thin and delicate, and, as is usual in such cases, the prosopyles are very clearly shown. Even the outermost Ascon-tubes generally retain their wide gastral cavity, so that the skin (pseudoderm) is formed out of the outer walls only of the outer tubes, strengthened by specially large spicules.

(*b.*) *Arrangement of the Skeleton.*—The skeleton consists of quadriradiate and triradiate spicules, arranged in a perfectly normal manner; the spicules in the pseudoderm are markedly larger than those inside the colony and the spicules in the oscular membrane have a strong tendency to become sagittal. The apical rays of the quadriradiates, of course, project freely into the gastral cavities of the Ascon-tubes.

(*c.*) *The Spicules.*—As these vary somewhat in different specimens, especially in size, I propose to give separate accounts of the spiculation of four specimens, which we may call A, B, C and D, and in this way to give a fair idea of the extent of variation. The spicules of the two extreme forms (A and D) are figured (Pl. X., Figs. 1, 2.)

Specimen A. (Pl. X., Fig. 1.)

(1.) *Triradiates.*—*Dermal.* Regular; rays conical, fairly gradually sharp-pointed, measuring about 0·15 by 0·014 mm. *Deep.* Of the same form as the dermal spicules but with smaller and slenderer rays, measuring 0·11 by 0·0085 mm.

---

* Possibly stained by other specimens in the same jar with the sponge.

(2.) *Quadriradiates.*—Abundant. Of the same size and shape as the deep triradiates except for the usually perfectly straight apical ray projecting from the centre at right angles to the facial rays. The apical ray is well developed and gradually and very sharply pointed, but not quite so long as the facial rays and a trifle slenderer.

In the oscular membrane many of the spicules are markedly sagittal.

Specimen B.

(1.) *Triradiates.—Dermal.* Regular; rays conical or slightly fusiform, gradually sharp-pointed, measuring about 0·24 by 0·03 mm. *Deep.* Regular; rays slender, conical, fairly sharp-pointed, measuring about 0·14 by 0·01 mm.

(2.) *Quadriradiates.*—Of about the same size and shape as the deep triradiates, but with an apical ray projecting at right angles from the centre. The apical ray is usually straight, slightly fusiform, not quite so long as the facials, very slender and finely pointed.

In the oscular membrane the spicules often become beautifully sagittal, both quadriradiates and triradiates having the oral rays curved backwards towards the basal ray, which is rather longer than the orals. (Here, and in the other specimens also, the spicules of the oscular fringe are of about the same size as the deep triradiates.)

Specimen C.

(1.) *Triradiates.—Dermal.* (*a*) Regular, large and stout; rays conical or subfusiform, gradually sharp-pointed, measuring about 0·25 by 0·035 mm. (*b*) Sagittal, occurring in small numbers around some of the pseudopores and probably also in the oscular membrane. These are approximately equiangular and the rays are about equal in length, but the oral rays are curved symmetrically, while the basal ray is straight. Rays conical, sharp-pointed, measuring about 0·1 by 0·01 mm. *Deep.* Regular; rays slender, conical or slightly fusiform, sharp-pointed, measuring about 0·15 by 0·014 mm.

(2.) *Quadriradiates.*—These are scarce and also of two forms. (*a*) Regular, like the deep triradiates in shape and size but with a straight, slender apical ray projecting from the centre. (*b*) Sagittal, found in the oscular membrane and (?)around some of the pseudopores; much like the sagittal triradiates in size and shape but with a long and well-developed, though slender apical ray, curving gradually upwards, sickle-like, from the centre of the spicule and gradually and finely pointed.

Specimen D. (Pl. X., Fig. 2.)

(1) *Triradiates.—Dermal.* Regular, large and stout. Rays conical or slightly fusiform, gradually and sharply pointed, measuring 0·3 by 0·035 mm., or a little less. *Deep.* Regular, rays slender, conical, fairly sharp-pointed, measuring about 0·14 by 0·0085 mm.

(2.) *Quadriradiates.*—Of about the same size and shape as the deep triradiates, but with an apical ray projecting at right angles from the centre. The apical ray is usually straight, not quite so long as the others, very slender and finely pointed, slightly fusiform. There are also a few larger quadriradiates amongst the dermal spicules.

The spicules of the oscular membrane are, as usual, distinctly sagittal, with backwardly curved oral rays.

From the above details it will be seen that the variation in spiculation concerns chiefly the dermal triradiates, the rays of which range from 0·15 by 0·014 to 0·3 by 0·035 mm., and the quadriradiates, which are sometimes scarce and sometimes abundant, with the apical ray variously developed. In all specimens the spicules of the oscular membrane tend to become markedly sagittal and a similar state of things is sometimes observable around the pseudopores.

(*d.*) *Affinities.*—This species would come, of course, under the genus *Ascaltis* of Hæckel's system, but I know of no other species which resembles it sufficiently closely to demand special notice. The sagittal triradiates and quadriradiates in the neighbourhood of the oscula appear to be very characteristic.

(*e.*) *Locality.*—Near Port Phillip Heads. (Coll. J. B. Wilson.)

8. *Leucosolenia cavata*, Carter, sp.

(Pl. II., Fig. 7 ; Pl. V. Figs. 1, 2 ; Pl. VI., Figs. 4, 5 ; Pl. IX., Fig. 4.)

Clathrina cavata, Carter. Annals and Magazine of Natural History, June, 1886, p. 502.

(*a.*) *General Appearance and Canal System.*—The sponge (Pl. II., Fig. 7) forms massive colonies of considerable size and with a fairly even surface. The colony grows vertically upwards, and is conspicuously flattened on the top and generally also more or less flattened from side to side, sometimes very much so. The lowest portion of the colony, attached to the substratum, consists of a number of separate, slender Ascon-tubes ; the greater part is, however, enclosed in a common external skin (pseudoderm) pierced by the numerous, closely placed pseudopores. The pseudopores are nearly circular and rather small, ranging up to about 0·54 mm. in diameter, they are abundant on the sides of the sponge but rare on the upper surface. On the upper, flattened surface of the colony are numerous good-sized oscula, each surrounded by a very well developed oscular fringe, and averaging about 3 mm. in diameter. The largest specimen in the collection is represented in Figure 7, Plate II. It is about 110 mm. in height, and over 50 mm. in its lesser horizontal diameter at the top. Unfortunately the specimen had to be cut to make it go into the bottle, so its greater horizontal diameter cannot be determined. The colour in spirit is white.

Full details of the canal-system are given on pp. 29, 30. It belongs to the "reversed" type (type C) and is illustrated in Figures 1, 2, Plate V. The peculiar "yellow granules," which seem to be characteristic of the species, are described and their nature discussed on p. 18 et seq. (Pl. VI., Figs. 4, 5.)

(b.) *Arrangement of the Skeleton.*—The skeleton consists mainly of triradiate spicules lying in a rather confused layer in the mesoderm (Pl. VI., Fig. 5). A good many quadriradiates are also present, with the apical rays as usual projecting into the gastral cavities of the Ascon-tubes. A very few oxeotes also occur in boiled out preparations.

(c.) *The Spicules* (Pl. IX., Fig. 4).

- (1) *Triradiates.*—*Dermal.* Regular. Rays conical, tapering a little more suddenly towards the apex, which is fairly sharp, measuring about 0·16 by 0·014 mm. *Deep.* The same as the dermal, but with the rays perhaps a little stouter.
- (2.) *Quadriradiates.*—Like the triradiates but with a small apical ray, which is slender, gradually sharply pointed and slightly curved.
- (3.) *Oxeotes.*—These are rare, small, asymmetrically fusiform, generally slightly and irregularly curved, measuring about 0·2 by 0.0083 mm.

(d.) *Affinities.*—Mr. Carter's description of this species is not very satisfactory, as he mistook the true nature of the arrangement of the canal system, stating that the oscula are "*only* in communication with the *dilated parts* of the interspaces," whereas, as we have seen, they are really true oscula and what Mr. Carter considered as interspaces are gastral cavities. The very peculiar reversal of the canal system is extremely misleading, and this doubtless gave rise to Mr. Carter's error. Comparison with a piece of one of Mr. Carter's type specimens kindly sent to me from the British Museum has convinced me that my specimens are identical with Mr. Carter's *Clathrina cavata.*

I have already indicated the possible identity of *Leucosolenia cavata* with *L. dubia* in the description of the latter. The species is common near Port Phillip Heads.

(c.) *Locality.*—Near Port Phillip Heads. (Coll. J. B. Wilson.)

9. *Leucosolenia protogenes*, Hæckel sp.

(Pl. III., Fig. 1; Pl. XI., Fig. 1.)

Ascetta primordialis, var. *protogenes*, Hæckel. "Die Kalkschwämme," Vol. II., p. 17.

Ascetta procumbens, von Lendenfeld. Proceedings of the Linnean Society of New South Wales, Vol. IX., Part 4, p. 1086.

Clathrina primordialis, Carter, Annals and Magazine of Natural History, June, 1886, p. 510.

(a.) *General Appearance and Canal System.*—The colony (Pl. III., Fig. 1) forms large, irregularly rounded, lobose masses, sometimes attaining a diameter of as much as 125 mm. and attached by the lower surface to the substratum. The texture of the colony is characteristically soft, spongy and friable. The surface of the colony is thrown into strong, irregular, rounded ridges and depressions. The pseudopores are much more abundant in the depressed portions of the surface than on the ridges, where the outer skin (pseudoderm) is better developed; they are irregularly rounded or oval in shape and measure about 1 mm. in maximum diameter. On the upper surface of the colony are numerous large circular pseudoscula, arranged along the tops of the ridges and each with a rather feebly developed membranous collar surrounding it. The pseudoscula measure about 6 mm. in diameter and lead each into a distinct, tubular pseudogaster which penetrates deeply into the substance of the colony. The colour in spirit is nearly white.

The canal system conforms to type D, and hence agrees with that of *Leucosolenia ventricosa*, which will be found described on pp. 30, 31, and illustrated in Figure 4, Plate IV.

(b.) *Arrangement of the Skeleton.*—The skeleton consists of triradiate spicules only, and these are arranged in the normal manner; in a dense, confused layer, with freely overlapping rays in the pseudoderm, and less densely packed in the walls of the internal Ascon-tubes.

(c.) *The Spicules* (Pl. XI., Fig. 1).—Triradiates only, of slightly different size and shape according to whether they lie in the pseudoderm or in the deeper parts of the colony. *Dermal.* These are equiradiate and equiangular (regular), fairly sharply pointed; the rays are almost cylindrical till pretty near the apex when they begin to taper off gradually, they measure about 0·14 by 0·0136 mm. *Deep.* Like the preceding but with slenderer rays measuring about 0·14 by 0.009 mm. Numerous very small triradiates occur amongst these as in other species and as figured by Hæckel for *Ascetta primordialis*; these are doubtless young forms. The spicules of the pseudoscular fringe and of the membrane which lines the pseudogaster resemble the ordinary deep-seated triradiates.

(d.) *Affinities.*—The identification of the four large specimens of this species in the collection with Carter's *Clathrina primordialis* is a safe one, because not only have I his long, published description and manuscript figures to go by, but also a piece of one of his own types from the British Museum. Mr. Carter's identification of his specimens with Hæckel's *Ascetta primordialis* is more open to doubt but appears to me to hold good if restricted to Hæckel's variety *Ascetta primordialis* var. *protogenes*, although in our specimens the dermal spicules are slightly thicker than the deep ones. I do not however place any great importance on so slight a distinction, although the specimens thereby make an approach to Hæckel's *Ascetta primordialis* var. *poterium* with its stout dermal spicules.

Poléjaeff records in the case of the specimens in the "Challenger" collection identified by him as *Leucosolenia poterium* (?) the presence of sagittal spicules in the pseudoscular membrane. I have found none such in my specimens of *Leucosolenia protogenes*.

Hæckel's *Ascetta primordialis* var. *protogenes* includes of course specimens with various types of canal system, but I propose to admit the specific, or at any rate varietal, identity only of forms with the same type of canal system, and hence the nomenclature becomes a matter of considerable difficulty. In the absence of definite information as to the canal system of the original type of *protogenes* I propose at present to restrict the name to specimens which conform to my type D of the *Reticulata*.

My reason for considering that von Lendenfeld's *Ascetta procumbens* is synonymous with *Leucosolenia protogenes* is that I have examined a fragment of one of his type specimens from Port Jackson, sent to me from the British Museum, and can find no points of distinction. Von Lendenfeld says, *loc. cit.*—" Our species is distinguished from the allied species by the rays of the spicules being neither cylindrical as in Ascetta coriacea nor pointed as in the numerous varieties of Ascetta primordialis. Besides that, the spicules are shorter than in the latter and thicker than in the former." The fragment (named by Dr. von Lendenfeld) examined by me shows nothing distinctive in the spiculation, and I should certainly say that the spicules, at any rate many of them, are pointed. In his description of *Ascetta procumbens*, von Lendenfeld says—" The sponge consists of numerous slightly curved cylindrical tubes, extending in one plane in one or more layers. The sponge has the appearance of a perforated plate, and attains a diameter of 25 and a thickness of 2·5 mm." One of his figures (Pl. LXI., Fig. 1a) agrees with this description, but three others, said to be of the same species (Pl. LXI., Figs, 1b, 1c, 1d), represent a massive, lobose sponge of very different appearance. The fragment also, sent to me from the British Museum, is evidently a portion of a massive sponge. Hence it seems not impossible that von Lendenfeld has confused two species, the description of the external form and spicules being taken from specimens which may perhaps differ from *Leucosolenia protogenes*. The canal system is not properly described, nor is the fragment in my possession sufficiently perfect to allow me to completely elucidate it, but this fragment so closely resembles, in all the characteristics which it exhibits, the Victorian specimens of *Leucosolenia protogenes*, that I have little hesitation in identifying it. Moreover, von Lendenfeld gives Port Phillip as a locality for his *Ascetta procumbens*.

(c.) *Locality.*—Near Port Phillip Heads. (Coll. J. B. Wilson.)

10. *Leucosolenia ventricosa*, Carter, sp.

(Pl. I., Figs. 8, 9, 10; Pl. IV., Fig. 4; Pl. X., Fig. 4.)

Clathrina ventricosa, Carter, Annals and Magazine of Natural History, June, 1886, p. 512.

(a.) *General Appearance and Canal System.*—The sponge (Pl. I., Figs. 8, 9, 10) forms large, irregularly lobose masses with nearly even or very uneven surface, each colony forming a thick wall around a very large pseudogaster which penetrates to the base of the sponge. Several such colonies may occur more or less fused together side by side, each with its large pseudogaster. Well-grown specimens measure about 75 mm. in height and the same in diameter. Each pseudogaster opens at the top of the colony through a wide pseudosculum surrounded by an extension of the lining membrane of the pseudogaster in the form of a pseudoscular fringe. The pseudopores are thickly and pretty evenly distributed in the pseudoderm, varying in size up to about 1 mm. in diameter, and mostly of oval shape.

From the lower surface of the colony short, root-like processes are given off which attach the sponge to the substratum on which it grows. The colour in spirit is white and the texture of the sponge is characteristically harsh and unyielding to the touch.

The canal system conforms to type D, and is described in detail on pp. 30, 31, and illustrated in Fig. 4, Plate IV.

(b.) *Arrangement of the Skeleton.*—The skeleton consists of triradiate, quadriradiate and oxeote spicules. The triradiates form nearly the entire skeleton and are arranged in an irregular layer in the walls of the Ascon-tubes and in an especially dense layer of especially large spicules mixed with smaller ones in the pseudoderm. The quadriradiates are relatively few but easily discoverable and even abundant in some specimens, they occur in the walls of the Ascon-tubes, with the apical ray projecting into the gastral cavity, and in the lining membrane of the pseudogaster with the apical ray projecting into the latter. The oxeote spicules vary greatly as to the numbers in which they occur in different specimens. Their position, however, appears to be constant. They have one end embedded in the margin of the pseudopore, while the greater part of the spicule projects freely, sometimes singly and sometimes in dense tufts, towards the centre of the pseudopore. In some specimens the pseudopores literally bristle with these tufts of oxeotes converging towards but not reaching the centre of the space, in others only a few oxeotes can be found.

(c.) *The Spicules* (Pl. X., Fig. 4).

(1.) *Triradiates.*—*Dermal.* Regular; rays conical or subfusiform, gradually sharp-pointed, very stout, measuring about 0·35 by 0·056 mm. (Numerous smaller spicules occur mixed with these.) *Deep.* Regular; rays conical or subfusiform, gradually sharp-pointed, measuring 0·17 by 0·014 mm. Numerous intermediate sizes occur.

(2.) *Quadriradiates.*—Of the same shape and size as the smaller triradiates, but with a short, slender, curved and sharply pointed apical ray.

Sometimes the smaller spicules in the pseudoscular membrane become strongly sagittal, the oral rays being curved backwards towards the basal.

(3.) *Oxeotes.*—Short, slender, straight, gradually sharply pointed at both ends, measuring about 0·16 by 0·003 mm.

(d.) *Affinities.*—This species, which Mr. Carter characterises as "by far the largest and most abundant in specimens of all Mr. Wilson's calcareous sponges" is easily recognisable by both general appearance and spiculation. Mr. Carter makes no mention of the oxeote spicules, but as I find them present in one of his type specimens sent to me from the British Museum this must be an oversight on his part.

(*c.*) *Locality.*—Near Port Phillip Heads. (Coll. J. B. Wilson.)

10A. *Leucosolenia ventricosa* var. *solida*, nov.
(Plate III., Fig. 8.)

This variety, represented in the collection by two good specimens, differs from the typical form in the flattened, cake-like shape and the suppression of the pseudogaster. The exhalant canal system is reduced to a shallow pit varying up to about a quarter of an inch in diameter, in the bottom of which are visible several small circular openings (exhalant openings of the Ascon-tubes). Around this pit there is a slightly-developed fringe. Numerous pits of this kind occur on the upper surface of each specimen. It is doubtful whether one is justified any longer in speaking of a pseudogaster and pseudosculum in this variety, for the collared cells appear to approach very closely to the edge of the pit, at any rate in some cases. Perhaps it would be better to regard the pits as groups of true oscula or even each as a single true osculum formed by the union of many Ascon-tubes. Hence the canal system is referable rather to type B than to type D.

In spiculation this form is identical with *Leucosolenia ventricosa* as described above, and as the spiculation is very characteristic I therefore regard it as a well-marked variety of that species.

Locality.—Near Port Phillip Heads. (Coll. J. B. Wilson.)

Subsection 2. *Subdivisa.*

The gastral cavities of the Ascon-tubes are more or less subdivided into chambers by ingrowths of mesoderm or of both mesoderm and endoderm.

11. *Leucosolenia proxima*, n. sp.
(Pl. II., Figs. 1, 2; Pl. VIII., Figs. 1, 2, 3, 4; Pl. XI., Fig. 2).

(*a.*) *General Appearance and Canal System.*—The sponge forms small colonies attached by little, solid, root-like processes to foreign objects (*e.g. Polyzoa*). The form of the colony is irregular and somewhat variable and will be best understood by reference to Figures 1, 2, Plate II., representing two slight varieties in one of which the oval pseudopores are conspicuously larger than in the other. On the upper surface of the colony are numerous conical projections, each having a small osculum at its summit. The greatest diameter of a colony is usually only about 6 or 7 mm. The colour in spirit is nearly white.

The canal system belongs to type E. and is fully described on pp. 32, 33 and illustrated in Figures 1, 2, Plate VIII.

(b.) *Arrangement of the Skeleton.*—The skeleton consists of triradiate spicules only, arranged as usual in the thickness of the mesoderm, the dermal spicules being larger than the deep ones.

(c.) *The Spicules* (Pl. XI., Fig. 2).—*Dermal.* Regular; rays stout, conical, gradually and sharply pointed, measuring about 0·16 by 0.021 mm. *Deep.* Similar to the dermal spicules but with the rays shorter and scarcely half as stout.

(d.) *Affinities.*—Were it not for the peculiar ingrowth of the mesoderm into the gastral cavities this species would present no peculiarity and would come near to *Leucosolenia pulcherrima;* as it is it forms a very interesting connecting link between the species with simple gastral cavities (*Indivisa*) and such forms as *Leucosolenia wilsoni.*

(e.) *Locality.*—Near Port Phillip Heads. (Coll. J. B. Wilson.)

12. *Leucosolenia wilsoni,* n. sp.

(Pl. II., Figs 3, 3a, 4; Pl. VII.; Pl. XI., Fig. 3.)

(a.) *General Appearance and Canal System.*—The sponge forms a low-growing, much flattened, spreading mass (Pl. II., Figs. 3, 4), sometimes growing out into rounded lobes (as at *x* in Figure 4). From the lower surface arise a few short, root-like processes which serve to attach the sponge to the substratum. On the upper surface, at irregular intervals, occur small conical papillæ, each with a minute osculum at its apex. On the upper surface the pseudopores are mostly elongated, narrow and slit-like, on the lower surface they are more rounded. The greatest horizontal diameter of the single adult specimen in the collection was about 35 mm. and its thickness very variable. In spirit the specimen has a characteristic dead white, solid appearance, due to the partial filling up of the Ascon-tubes.

The canal system (Pl. VII., Figs. 1, 2, 3) belongs to type F and is fully described on p. 34. The developing embryos are contained in separate spherical cavities lined by very large, polygonal, plate-like cells (Pl. VII., Fig. 3).

(*b.*) *Arrangement of the Skeleton.*—The skeleton consists of triradiate spicules only, arranged as usual in the thickness of the mesoderm and often, especially in the thick pseudoderm, in several layers.

(*c.*) *The Spicules* (Pl. XI., Fig. 3).—*Dermal.* Regular triradiates; rays stout, conical, gradually sharp-pointed, measuring about 0.14 by 0.014 mm., or a trifle stouter. *Deep.* Like the dermal spicules but with the rays a little shorter and slenderer, still fairly stout.

(*d.*) *Affinities.*—This species obviously comes very near to Hæckel's *Ascetta primordialis* var. *loculosa*[*] but it is no easy matter to determine what *Ascetta primordialis* var. *loculosa* really is, as the name is evidently applied by Hæckel to a number of forms which differ widely in canal system and must therefore, according to our view, be considered as distinct species.

Ascetta loculosa, H. (*Ascetta primordialis* var. *loculosa*) is diagnosed by Hæckel as follows :—" Spicula alle von gleicher Grösse, einer doppelte oder mehrfache Schicht im Exoderm bildend, ihre Strahlen 8-16 mal so lang als dick. Entoderm verdickt, ein geschichtetes Epithelium bildend, welches durch blattförmige Fortsätze oder Septa die Darmhöhle in Fächer abtheilt. (*Australien*)." As it is placed in the genus *Ascetta* the spicules are, of course, all triradiate. The only further description given by Hæckel of the remarkable species or variety *loculosa* is as follows :—" Eine andere sehr bemerkenswerthe Varietät, die ich anfangs für eine ganz verschiedene Art hielt, bekam ich aus Südaustralien (*Ascetta loculosa*). Hier war sowohl Exoderm als Entoderm verdickt. Das Exoderm enthielt mehrfache Nadelschichten und bildete dünne membranoese Vorsprünge und Scheidewände inneshalb der Darmröhren, durch welche dieselben in Fächer abgetheilt wurden. Diese Scheidewände enthielten keine Spicula und trugen ein aus mehreren Schichten von Epithelzellen gebildetes Entoderm. Bei einigen Stöcken fand sich in jedem Fach ein reifer Embryo, ganz ähnlich wie bei *Ascetta clathrus*, wo dies Verhältniss genauer beschrieben werden wird (vgl. Taf. 4, Fig. 4-7). Die Stöcke von Ascetta loculosa, welche solche Fächer in der Darmhöhle enthielten, würden im künstlichen System zu vier verschiedenen Gattungen gehört haben, nämlich Soleniscus, Tarrus, Auloplegma und Ascometra."

Probably our *Leucosolenia wilsoni* is identical with one or other of the forms included by Hæckel under the name *Ascetta loculosa*, although without more exact information as to the latter it is difficult to be certain of this. But, granting that it is so, the question of nomenclature is still by no means settled, as we have to decide

[*] " Die Kalkschwämme," Vol. II., pp. 17, 23.

to which of the various forms included by Hæckel under the name *loculosa* that name should be restricted. None of these forms are figured and none are specially described, but the first mentioned is the *Soleniscus*, hence I propose to restrict the name *loculosa* to a *Soleniscus* form. It must be remembered, in considering Hæckel's account, that his term "*Exoderm*" includes both ectoderm and mesoderm. Although Hæckel found embryos he does not appear to have noticed the curious embryocapsules which are so conspicuous in *Leucosolenia wilsoni*, perhaps they do not occur in any of Hæckel's forms, if so they might form a distinctive character for *Leucosolenia wilsoni*.

Hæckel's *Ascetta clathrina*[*] also exhibits the same peculiarity in regard to the subdivision of the Ascon-tubes by ingrowths of mesoderm and endoderm ("endogastriche Septa," Hk.), but in that species, which Hæckel regards as a variety of *Ascetta clathrus*, the rays of the spicules are knobbed at the extremities.

The affinities of *Leucosolenia wilsoni* to *L. proxima* have already been indicated in describing the latter species.

(c.) *Locality*.—Near Port Phillip Heads. (Coll. J. B. Wilson.)

13. *Leucosolenia depressa*, n. sp.

(Pl. III., Figs. 4, 4a; Pl. VIII., Fig. 8; Pl. XI., Fig. 4.)

(a.) *General Appearance and Canal System*.—The single specimen (Pl. III., Figs. 4, 4a) forms a flattened, spreading, irregular crust, attached to the substratum (if at all) at a few points only. The greatest diameter of the specimen is a little over 100 mm. and the average thickness about 10 mm. or less. The surface is smooth but irregular and undulating. On the upper surface are scattered numerous very small, conical papillæ, each with a very minute osculum at its summit. On the upper surface also the pseudoderm is very strongly developed, with comparatively few, small pseudopores scattered in irregular patches here and there. On the under surface, on the other hand, the pseudopores are larger and thickly scattered all over, giving to it a sieve-like appearance. In spirit the colour of the sponge is greyish white.

The canal system is like that of *Leucosolenia wilsoni* (type F), but with the ingrowths into the gastral cavities of the Ascon-tubes more irregular and less strongly developed, consisting principally of irregular proliferations of the endoderm.

[*] "Die Kalkschwämme," Vol. 2, p. 31.

(b.) *Arrangement of the Skeleton.*—The skeleton consists of triradiate and quadriradiate spicules arranged irregularly in one or more layers in the thickness of the mesoderm.

(c.) *The Spicules* (Pl. XI., Fig. 4).

(1) *Triradiates.*—Regular. *Dermal.* Large and stout; rays conical or slightly fusiform, gradually sharp-pointed, measuring about 0·2 by 0·028 mm. *Deep.* Rays long and rather slender, fairly gradually and sharply pointed, measuring about 0·14 by 0·008 mm.

(2) *Quadriradiates.*—These spicules are abundant, they resemble the deep triradiates but have a feebly developed apical ray.

(d.) *Affinities.*—I at first regarded this sponge as a variety of *Leucosolenia wilsoni*, which it closely resembles in external appearance and in canal system, but considering the differences in spiculation it is perhaps better for the present to regard it as a distinct species. The specimen contains numerous unsegmented ova[*], in the same position as the embryos in *L. wilsoni*, but there is no special epithelial capsule visible around them, perhaps this is developed only after segmentation.

(e.) *Locality.*—Near Port Phillip Heads. (Coll. J. B. Wilson.)

Section 3. *Radiata.*

The sponge consists of a single central Ascon-tube from which smaller tubes are budded off radially.

14. *Leucosolenia tripodifera*, Carter, sp.

(Pl. II., Figs. 5, 6; Pl. V., Figs. 3, 4; Pl. VIII., Figs. 5, 6; Pl. XI., Fig. 5.)

Leucetta clathrata, Carter, Annals and Magazine of Natural History, 1883, Vol. XI., p. 33.

Clathrina tripodifera, Carter, Annals and Magazine of Natural History, June, 1886, p. 505.

Clathrina tripodifera var. *gravida*, Carter, *loc. cit.*, p. 507.

(a.) *General Appearance and Canal System.*—As I have already given a full

[*] Described on pp. 17, 18.

account of the external form and canal system of this remarkable sponge on pp. 35, 36, I need only refer the reader to that description and to the illustrations (Pl. II., Figs. 5, 6; Pl. V., Figs. 3, 4; Pl. VIII., Figs. 5, 6) and pass on to describe the arrangement of the skeleton and the form of the spicules.*

(*b.*) *Arrangement of the Skeleton.*—The skeleton consists of rather slender sagittal triradiates and quadriradiates and of the "tripod" spicules (triradiate). The triradiates and quadriradiates are arranged in a single layer, though of course with frequently overlapping rays, in the mesoderm of the walls of the tubes, the quadriradiates with the apical ray projecting freely into the gastral cavity (Pl. V., Fig. 4). As already stated the spicules are sagittal, and in the central Ascon-tube the basal ray points towards the base of the sponge, while in the radiating tubes the basal ray is directed towards the outer, blind end of the tube just as in the articular tubar skeleton of the Sycons. The "tripod" spicules form a protective layer on the outside of the colony, being placed at the blind ends of the radiating tubes with all three rays pointing inwards (Pl. V., Fig. 4).

(*c.*) *The Spicules* (Pl. XI., Fig. 5).

(1.) *Triradiates.—Dermal.* These are the "tripod" spicules and the extent to which they are developed varies in different specimens. When fully developed the rays are very stout and curved towards one another in such a manner that if the spicule were placed with the apices of the rays resting on a level surface the centre of the spicule would lie very much above that surface; towards their apices the rays curve outwards again. Rays stout, conical, gradually but not very sharply pointed, measuring about 0·12 by 0.02 mm. *Deep.* Sagittal, rays long and slender; angles about equal; rays straight, or nearly so, fairly gradually and fairly sharply pointed. Basal ray longer than the orals, averaging, say, about 0·16 by 0·0095 mm. when the orals measure about 0·1 by 0·0075 mm., but the size of these spicules is subject to a good deal of variation.

(2.) *Quadriradiates.*—Like the deep triradiates but with longer and slenderer facial rays and with the addition of a shorter apical ray generally rather strongly and often suddenly curved upwards. In a well developed example the basal ray measures about 0·24 by 0·005 mm. and the orals about 0·21 by 0·005 mm., but here again there is a good deal of variation, especially in the development of the apical ray.

(*d.*) *Affinities.* —I have a good many specimens of this species, which is very

---

* I may add that the colour of the sponge in spirit is grey, or nearly white, and the texture rather soft and delicate. The peculiar structure of the endoderm is described on p. 11.

easily to be recognised. Curiously enough Mr. Carter, in his original description, makes no mention of the sagittal character exhibited by most of the spicules, but this character is very clearly shown in a portion of one of his types of the species sent to me from the British Museum; to such an extent, indeed, that the oral rays are sometimes slightly recurved towards the basal, in addition to being markedly shorter.

The only other species which could possibly be included amongst the Homocœla radiata is von Lendenfeld's *Homoderma sycandra*[*], indeed his diagnosis of the *Homodermidæ*, viz., " Homocœla with radial tubes " would serve very well for the radiate section of the genus *Leucosolenia*. His figures of *Homoderma*, however, and especially of the collared cells, are so exceedingly diagrammatic and his description of the histology so scanty that, as stated previously, I must agree with Vosmaer[†] in regarding the matter as still *sub judice*. Even if *Homoderma sycandra* be a Homocœlous sponge still it is totally different from *Leucosolenia tripodifera*, conforming as it does in every particular except the problematical extension of the collared cells into the gastral cavity, to the normal *Sycon* type with unbranched radial tubes (flagellated chambers).

Unfortunately I have not had the opportunity of examining a specimen of Carter's *Clathrina tripodifera* var. *gravida*,[‡] but there seems no doubt that it really is a slight variety of *Leucosolenia tripodifera*; the only doubt seems to be whether it deserves a special varietal name. The variety was represented by a single very small specimen with several oscula; according to Mr. Carter's description there are no quadriradiate spicules present, but in an unpublished illustration of the variety which he has kindly sent me a quadriradiate spicule of the usual form is figured; another difference lies in the more slender character of the rays of the internal triradiates in the variety *gravida*. An unfortunate complication in nomenclature arises from Mr. Carter's statement after the description of this variety (*loc. cit.*):—
" There can be no doubt that this is the same sponge as, only in a larger form than, that which I described and illustrated under the name of ' *Leucetta clathrata* ' (' Annals', 1883, Vol. XI., p. 33; Pl. I., Figs. 13—17)." As the name *clathrus* has already been used for a species of *Leucosolenia*§ and as the original description of *Leucetta clathrata* was so imperfect we may perhaps with advantage retain Mr. Carter's later name *tripodifera* for the species under consideration, in preference to reverting to the name which seems to have a prior claim.

(c.) *Localities.*—Near Port Phillip Heads. (Coll. J. B. Wilson); Westernport (Victoria), Kent Islands (Bass Straits). (Coll. J. Gabriel.)

[*] Proceedings of the Linnean Society of New South Wales, Vol. IX., Part 4, p. 1089. *Vide* also p. 70 of this memoir.
[†] Bronn's " Klassen und Ordnungen des Thierreichs." " Porifera," p. 387.
[‡] Annals and Magazine of Natural History, June, 1886, p. 507.
[§] *Vide* Haeckel, " Die Kalkschwämme," Vol. II., p. 30. (*Ascetta clathrus*).

Doubtful Species.

For the sake of completeness it is proposed in this place to quote the original descriptions of those Victorian sponges which have been described as Homoccela (or Ascones), but concerning which we are not at present in possession of sufficient information to make identification and classification, without examination of the original specimens, which is at present impossible, a matter of anything like certainty.

I may mention here that I have carefully examined a fragment of Mr. Carter's "*Clathrina latitubulata* (provisional, incertæ sedis)"[*] sent by Mr. Carter to the British Museum and thence to me, and that I find it to be an undoubted Sycon with small, but branched, flagellated chambers (radial tubes).

1. *Leucosolenia osculum*, Carter, sp.

Clathrina osculum, Carter, Annals and Magazine of Natural History. June, 1886, p. 503.

"Individualised, social. Globular, stipitate, presenting on the summit a short, cylindrical, hollow process, and ending below in one or more filiform stems fixed to the object on which it has grown, composed throughout of a mass of tubulated thread-like filament growing by almost infinite and irregular branching and anastomosis into the form above mentioned. Colour sponge—brown when fresh, when dry dark grey. Surface even, uniformly reticulate, interstices about 1-120th in. in diameter. Pores numerous, passing *through* the wall of the hollow thread. Vent single, tubulated, at the summit of the specimen, composed of a thin, cylindrical extension of the *walls of the tubulation*, which at this part opens into it by a plurality of holes, and thus enters into its composition. No definite cloacal dilatation. Structure already stated, composed of the same kind of staple thread as *C. curata*, but smaller and more compact in its reticulation; wall of the tubulated thread very thin and skeletally composed of a single layer of triradiate spicules held together by sarcode, and lined by the softer parts, which here also appear to consist chiefly of a layer of spongozoa in juxtaposition, that is without being gathered into the form of ampullaceous sacs, together with a remarkable quantity of those organs which consist of nucleated cells respectively surrounded by an abundance of glistening spherical granules, which Häckel has figured and named 'nuclei' (Kerne) of the syncytium, as before stated. Stem apparently an extension of the tubulated thread, but more solid. Spicules of one kind only, viz., triradiates of different sizes, but for the most part equiarmed and equiangulated, intercrossing each other on the surface so as to give the interstices of the reticulation here a polygonal border; spicules more plentiful and *larger* than in *C. curata*, ray of the larger ones averaging 42 by 5-6000ths in. in its greatest dimensions. Size of individual, of which there are two joined together, about 5-24ths in. in diameter; stem about 1-24th in. long and 1-48th in. in diameter.

"*Obs.*—To what size this species might ultimately grow I am ignorant, but that above described appears to be very small. It is, however, amply large enough to show in the section that the tubular vent is the *outlet of the tubulated structure*, and that, although there is no absolutely cloacal dilatation, this is indicated by the reticulated structure in the centre immediately under the vent being more open than towards the circumference. In these two particulars, then, it differs from *C. curata*, not more so, perhaps, than in the size and abundance of its spicules, especially on the surface, whereby the thickness of the wall of the tubulation here appears to consist of a plurality of layers instead of one only as in *C. curata*. The tubulation is charged internally with *ova* in the unsegmented state, large, and presenting the germinal vesicle.

"Upon the authority of Häckel I have stated that the 'nuclei,' mentioned in the two last species, are in his 'syncytium;' but, entertaining a different view of their nature, I must refer the student for my explanation of this assumption to the 'Annals' of 1881, Vol. XIV., pp. 20 and 21. The species is very like Schmidt's *Nardoa reticulum* (Spong. Küste v. Algier, p. 28, Taf. V., Figs. 7 and 8)."

This species seems to me to be based on an insufficient number of specimens which may not impossibly be simply young forms, as, indeed, Mr. Carter's description suggests. The canal system, to judge from the description and from an unpublished illustration sent to me by Mr. Carter, belongs to my type B. of the Homoccela reticulata, and in this respect the sponge closely resembles

---
[*] Annals and Magazine of Natural History, June, 1886, p. 515.

Leucosolenia pulcherrima, with which species I should be inclined to identify it were it not for the great difference in the size of the spicules and the absence of any information as to the shape of the spicule-rays in *Leucosolenia osculum*.

The specimens upon which Mr. Carter's description is based formed part of the collection sent to him by Mr. J. Bracebridge Wilson from the neighbourhood of Port Phillip Heads.

2. *Leucosolenia* (?) *laminoclathrata*, Carter, sp.

Clathrina laminoclathrata, Carter. Annals and Magazine of Natural History. June, 1886, p. 509.

"Specimen a subcircular patch about ⅜in. in diameter and ⅛ in. thick, which has grown over a rocky substance. Clathrous, massive, sessile, spreading, lamino reticulate. Colour now (that is in its dry state) steel-grey. Surface even, smooth, reticulated by the clathrous holing of the structure generally, which here makes its appearance in the form of circular interstices of different sizes up to ⅛ in. in diameter. Pores in the lamina. No appearance of a vent or vents of any kind, *i.e.* spurious or real. Structure lamino-clathrous ; lamina solid, composed of a thin layer of radiate spicules supporting the sarcode and other soft parts. Spicules of one form only, viz. triradiate, equiarmed and equiangled, varying in size under 75-6000ths in. in diameter, ray alone about 45 by 5-6000ths in. Size above given.

"*Obs.* In this instance, which is unique among the calcareous sponges so far as I know, the tubulated staple thread of *Clathrina*, which so generally characterizes this genus, is replaced by a flat, solid, 'tape-like' form or staple, whose edge when cut presents no appearance of mesodermal structure or parenchyma whatever, although towards the angles of union, where of course the lamina branches off to form the clathrous structure of the mass, there is a small angular space left which bears a faint trace of parenchyma, and this seems to introduce us to what in this way will become so much more evident hereafter. It is represented among the non-calcareous sponges by '*Echinoclathria facus.*' ('Annals,' 1883, vol. XVI., p. 292.)

"In the next species that will be described, viz., *Clathrina primordialis*, the reticulated flat lamina of *C. laminoclathrata* appears to be replaced by a vermiculated *tube*, in which the walls are just as thin as the lamina of this species, but which tubulation by repeated branching, contortion, and anastomosis, all more or less in apposition, assumes the form of a solid mass of this kind of structure in which the intervals between the tubulation afford a much larger space for parenchymatous structure than in *C. laminoclathrata*; in short, wherein the quantity of parenchymatous structure is much greater."

The specimen here described was sent by Mr. Wilson from the neighbourhood of Port Phillip Heads to Mr. Carter. In considering the description we must remember that it is based upon a small, *dry* specimen, in which probably the walls of the Ascon-tubes had collapsed together so as to form a solid thread, so that very likely Mr. Carter was misled in this case precisely as he had been previously misled in the case of his *Leucetta clathrata* (*vide suprà* p. 68). Unfortunately I have neither specimens nor figures of the species to assist me in arriving at a true conclusion as to its real nature, but I think there can be little doubt that the species must be abandoned.

3. *Leucosolenia* (?) *sycandra*, von Lendenfeld, sp.

Homoderma sycandra, von Lendenfeld. Proceedings of the Linnean Society of New South Wales. Vol. IX., Part 4, p. 1088.

"Quadriradiate, triradiate and acerate spicules. The radial tubes in regular strobiloid circles around the cylindrical Gastral cavity which is clothed up to the margin of the Osculum with frilled flagellate cells. Gastral quadriradiates, centripetal radial ray 0·02—0·04 x 0·0024 conic, pointed and straight; lateral tangental ray slightly curved, convex outside 0·05 x 0·0036; longitudinal, aboral tangental ray 0·01 x 0·0038. Parenchymal triradiates; internal triradiates with unequal rays, radial centrifugal ray 0·048 x 0·0032 conic, sometimes protruding into the Gastral cavity. Tangental basal rays curved 0·0071—0·011 x 0·0048, convex towards the outer side often equatorially situated.

"Median triradiates regular, rays conic 0·048 x 0·003. Dermal rays similar in size and shape to the former on the summits of the radial tubes some triradiates are situated, the outer rays of which protrude beyond the surface. Dermal acerates protruding and leaning towards the Osculum under an angle of 45° 0·71 x 0·0071 mm., cylindrical, pointed, the centrifugal end abruptly pointed to a sharp point. Situated in groups of 10 to 12 on the summits of the radial tubes. Oscular acerates a longitudinal cylinder forming a kind of Oesophagus with a frill of horizontal acerates. The former slightly curved, convex on the inner side 0·57 x 0·0016, the latter 0·21 x 0·003 slightly concave to the front.

"Persons attaining a height of 14 mm., and a breadth of 5 mm.

"Homoderma Sycandra is connected with the Asconidæ by forms such as Ascaltis canariensis,[*] and Ascaltis Gegenbauri.[†]

"*Locality*: East coast of Australia, Port Jackson, south coast of Australia, Port Phillip, Von Lendenfeld."

In view of the meagreness of the above description and especially of the entire absence of histological details, and in spite of the elaborately diagrammatic figures which accompany it, I fear we must at present place *Homoderma sycandra* amongst the doubtful species. It remains to be proved that the collared cells really do extend beyond the limits of the radial tubes, if they do not then the sponge is an ordinary Sycon. It will be observed that the sponge, whatever it may be, differs widely in structure from *Leucosolenia tripodifera*.

[*] Hæckel. "Die Kalkschwämme," Vol. II., p. 52; Vol. III., Pl. IX., Fig. 1—3, Pl. X., Figs. 1a—1c.
[†] *Loc. cit.* Vol. II., p. 62; Vol. III., Pl. IX. Figs. 6—9; Pl. X., Figs. 5a—5d.

V.—DESCRIPTIONS OF PLATES.

PLATE I.

Figure 1.—*Leucosolenia lucasi.* Part of a colony ; x 6.

Figure 2.—*Leucosolenia stolonifer.* Part of a colony ; x 2.

Figure 3.—*Leucosolenia dubia.* Part of a colony ; x 4.

Figures 4, 5.—*Leucosolenia stipitata.* Two entire colonies; natural size.

Figure 6.—*Leucosolenia stipitata.* The same specimen as represented in Figure 4 ; x 15.

Figure 7.—*Leucosolenia pulcherrima.* An entire colony ; x 7.

Figure 8.—*Leucosolenia ventricosa.* A small colony ; x 3.

Figure 9.—*Leucosolenia ventricosa.* A good-sized colony ; natural size.

Figure 10.—*Leucosolenia ventricosa.* The same specimen as represented in Figure 9, but cut in half longitudinally to show the pseudogaster ; natural size.

PLATE II.

Figure 1, 2.—*Leucosolenia proxima.* Two entire colonies ; x 8.

Figure 3.—*Leucosolenia wilsoni.* Upper surface of the colony; x 2.

Figure 3a.—*Leucosolenia wilsoni.* A very young colony ; x 2.

Figure 4.—*Leucosolenia wilsoni.* Half of the specimen represented in Figure 3 divided transversely ; showing the cut surface and, at *x*, a lobular outgrowth with an osculum ; x 2.

Figure 5.—*Leucosolenia tripodifera.* Group of specimens attached to Algae, &c.; from a photograph ; natural size.

Figure 6.—*Leucosolenia tripodifera.* The largest specimen in the collection; from a photograph ; natural size.

Figure 7.—*Leucosolenia cavata.* Part of a large colony, seen from the side. (The specimen has been cut, and one of the cut surfaces is seen in perspective on the right.) From a photograph ; natural size.

PLATE III.

Figure 1.—*Leucosolenia protogenes.* Part of a large specimen; natural size.

Figure 2.—*Leucosolenia pelliculata.* A good-sized specimen; x 2.

Figure 3.—*Leucosolenia ventricosa,* var. *solida.* Part of a large colony; natural size.

Figure 4.—*Leucosolenia depressa.* Upper surface of the specimen; natural size.

Figure 4a.—*Leucosolenia depressa.* Lower surface of the specimen; natural size.

PLATE IV.

Figure 1.—*Leucosolenia lucasi.* The upper portion of a single Ascon-person, highly magnified. At the summit of the tube is shown the wide osculum *(o.)* and in the right hand upper portion of the figure a piece of the thin wall of the tube is supposed to be cut away so as to show the gastral cavity. The collared cells are coloured red and the spicules blue.

 a. r. Apical ray of quadriradiate spicule projecting into the gastral cavity.

 o. Osculum.

 o.x. Oxeote spicule projecting from the outer surface of the tube wall.

 pr. Prosopyle.

 ra. Triradiate and quadriradiate spicules lying in the thickness of the mesoderm.

Figure 2.—*Leucosolenia stipitata.* Vertical section, passing through the osculum, of the specimen represented in Figure 6, Plate I.; showing the arrangement of the canal system. For the sake of clearness the thickness of the walls of the Ascon-tubes is slightly exaggerated. The endoderm is coloured red. (Zeiss a_2, Oc. 2, Camera.)

 g.c. Gastral cavity.

 int. Interspace between Ascon-tubes

 o. Osculum.

 p. Pseudopore.

 pd. Pseudoderm.

Figure 3.—*Leucosolenia pulcherrima.* Vertical section, passing through an osculum, of the specimen represented in Figure 7, Plate I.; showing the arrangement of the canal system. The endoderm is coloured red. (Zeiss a_2, Oc. 2, Camera.)

 st. Stalk.

 Other lettering as in Figure 2.

Figure 4. *Leucosolenia ventricosa.* Vertical section, passing through the pseudosculum, of the small specimen represented in Figure 8, Plate I.; showing the arrangement of the canal system. The endoderm is coloured red. (Zeiss a_2, Oc. 2, Camera.)

    o. Opening of Ascon-tube into pseudogaster (=osculum in Figures 2 and 3).
    pd. The portion of the pseudoderm which forms the lining membrane of the pseudogaster.
    p.g. Pseudogaster.
    p.o. Pseudosculum.
    Other lettering as in Figure 2.

PLATE V.

Figure 1.—*Leucosolenia cavata.* A small colony cut in half vertically to show the arrangement of the canal system. Enlarged and slightly diagrammatic. In the lower portion of the figure are seen the narrow Ascon-tubes separated by wide interspaces: in the upper portion are seen the narrow, tubular, inhalant canals (=interspaces of the lower portion) separated by wide, irregular cavities (=merged gastral cavities of the Ascon-tubes) out of which the oscula open.

    a.t. Ascon-tubes in their primitive condition, forming the lowermost portion of the colony.
    a.t'. Gastral cavities of the Ascon-tubes merged into irregular spaces.
    int. Interspaces between Ascon-tubes.
    int'. Interspaces transformed into narrow inhalant canals.
    o. Osculum.
    p. Pseudopore leading into wide irregular interspace.
    p'. Pseudopore leading into narrow, tubular interspace.
    pd. Pseudoderm.

Figure 2.—*Leucosolenia cavata.* Simplified diagram, based upon Figure 1, to illustrate the reversal of the canal system. The endoderm is coloured red and the space occupied by the merged gastral cavities is coloured black (except where the endodermal lining is seen *en face*). For the sake of clearness all the tubes are represented as unbranched and running vertically instead of in every direction as they really do (*cf.* Figure 1). The transition between the normal and the reversed portions of the canal system takes place in the area marked *x*, where it will be seen that there are really no tubes at all but two systems of spaces separated by an undulating membrane.

Lettering as in Figure 1.

Figure 3.—*Leucosolenia tripodifera*. A small specimen the upper portion of which has been divided longitudinally so as to exhibit the arrangement of the canal system. The red colour indicates the distribution of the collared cells, which are visible wherever the central cavity or the radial tubes have been cut into. The figure also shows how the radial tubes originate as little hollow diverticula (*r′t′*) of the wall of the central cavity a short way below the osculum, at first unbranched but as they grow older (*r.t.*) branching freely.

g.c. Gastral cavity.

int. Interspaces between radial tubes.

o. Osculum.

op. Openings of radial tubes into gastral cavity.

r.t. Radial tubes.

r′.t′. Young radial tubes.

Figure 4.—*Leucosolenia tripodifera*. Small portion of a thin section along the radial tubes seen under a low power of the microscope. In the upper right-hand part of the section the tubes are not cut into and their walls are seen *en face*. Elsewhere the tubes are cut right through so as to show their walls only in section. The endoderm is coloured red and the spicules blue.

a. Anastomosis between two neighbouring radial tubes.

pr. Prosopyle.

t.s. Large "tripod" spicules protecting the blind outer ends of the radial tubes.

Other lettering as in Figure 3.

PLATE VI.

Figure 1.—*Leucosolenia stolonifer*. Small portion of a transverse section of the wall of an Ascon-person. The endoderm is coloured red and the spicules blue. (Zeiss C, Oc. 2.)

ap. r. Apical ray of quadriradiate spicule, projecting into the gastral cavity.
ect. Ectoderm.
end. Endoderm.
i.c. Inhalant canal.
mes. Mesoderm.
pr. Prosopyle.
st. c. Stellate cell of mesoderm.

Figure 2.—*Leucosolenia stolonifer.* The projecting apical ray of a quadriradiate spicule, enclosed in its cellular sheath. (Zeiss F, Oc. 2.)

ap. r. Apical ray.
c.c. Collared cells around the base of the spicule ray.
sp. s. Sheath of flattened endothelial cells around the spicule ray.

Figure 3.—*Leucosolenia stolonifer.* A multipolar connective tissue cell of the mesoderm (Zeiss. F, Oc. 2).

Figure 4.—*Leucosolenia cavata.* Vertical section of tube-wall (Zeiss F, Oc. 2).

c.c. Collared cells.
ect. Nucleus of ectoderm cell.
mes. Mesodermal ground-substance.
ov. Ovum, surrounded by other mesodermal cells.
sp. Spicule.
st. c. Stellate cell of mesoderm.
y. gr. Group of yellow granules.

Figure 5.—*Leucosolenia cavata.* Portion of tube-wall laid out flat and examined as a transparent object; the entire thickness is supposed to be in focus. (Zeiss F, Oc. 2.)

y. gr. 1. Young (solid) group of yellow granules.
y. gr. 2. Fully developed group of yellow granules with central space.

Other lettering as in Figure 4.

PLATE VII.

Anatomy and histology of *Leucosolenia wilsoni*. (Red=endoderm; blue= spicules).

Figure 1.—Part of a vertical transverse section of the specimen represented in Figure 3, Plate II.; showing the arrangement of the canal system. (Zeiss a_2, Oc. 2, Camera.)

    em. Embryo.
    g. c. Gastral cavities of Ascon-tubes, more or less subdivided by endogastric septa.
    int. Interspaces between Ascon-tubes.
    o. Osculum.
    p. Pseudopore.
    pd. Pseudoderm.
    r. Root-like process which attaches the sponge to the substratum.

Figure 2.—Part of a section of a single Ascon-tube more highly magnified (Zeiss C, Oc. 2, Camera); showing the subdivision of the gastral cavity by endogastric septa. The collared cells appear to form several layers in some places, but this is probably due chiefly, if not entirely, to the irregularity of the surface which the endoderm covers causing the latter to be often cut tangentially.

    ect. Ectoderm.
    e. s. Endogastric septum.
    g. c. Gastral cavity.
    st. c. Stellate cells in mesoderm.

Figure 3.—Section similar to that represented in Figure 2, but with the endogastric septa more developed and containing embryos lying in special cavities lined by large endothelial cells. (Zeiss C, Oc. 2, Camera.)

    em. Embryo.
    n. c. Nutriant endothelial cells forming the embryo-capsule.
    n'. c. An embryo capsule cut tangentially so as to show the polygonal form of the endothelial cells.
Other lettering as in Figure 2.

Figure 4. Ectodermal epithelium seen in a tangential section of an Ascon-tube. (Zeiss F, Oc. 2, Camera.)

Figure 5.—Small portion of a thin section of an Ascon-tube, showing how the collared cells spread in from the wall of the tube over the mesodermal ingrowths, thus forming with the latter the endogastric septa. (Zeiss F, Oc. 2.)

    c. c.   Collared cells.

    mes.   Mesoderm of the tube-wall.

    mes'.   Ingrowth of mesoderm into the gastral cavity.

PLATE VIII.

Figure 1.—*Leucosolenia proxima*. Vertical section of the specimen represented in Figure 1, Plate II.; showing the arrangement of the canal system. The endoderm is coloured red. (Zeiss a_3, Oc. 2, Camera.)

    g. c.   Gastral cavity of Ascon-tube.

    int.   Interspace between Ascon-tubes.

    o.   Osculum.

    p.   Pseudopore.

    pd.   Pseudoderm.

    r.   Root-like attaching process.

    st. c.   Stellate mesoderm cells forming a network in the gastral cavity.

Figure 2.—*Leucosolenia proxima*. A small portion of a section more highly magnified (Zeiss F, Oc. 2); showing part of the wall of an Ascon-tube and part of the network of stellate mesodermal cells in the gastral cavity.

    c. c.   Collared cells (collars and flagella completely retracted).

    ect.   Ectoderm.

    mes.   Mesodermal ground-substance.

    nu.   Nucleus of stellate cell.

    sp.   Spicule.

    st. c.   Network of stellate cells in the gastral cavity.

Figures 3, 4.—*Leucosolenia proxima*. Group of three collared cells and isolated collared cell. The collars are still extended but the flagella are withdrawn. (Zeiss F, Oc. 4.)

    col.   Collar.

    nu.   Nucleus.

Figure 5.—*Leucosolenia tripodifera.* Small portion of a section of the tube-wall, showing the arrangement of the collared cells and Sollas's membrane, with the rod-like bodies.

      c. c.   Collared cells.
      r. b.   Rod-like bodies.
      s. m.   Sollas's membrane.

Figure 6.—*Leucosolenia tripodifera.* Portion of a section similar to that represented in Figure 5. but more highly magnified.

      col.   Collar of collared cell.
      Other lettering as in Figure 5.

Figure 7.—*Leucosolenia pelliculata.* Section of an ovum (Zeiss F, Oc. 2).

      gr. b.   Granular body of the ovum.
      no.   Nucleolus.
      nu.   Nucleus.

Figure 8.—*Leucosolenia depressa.* Section of an ovum (Zeiss F, Oc. 2). The outline of the section is indicated by a dotted line, the granular body of the ovum being filled in only at one place.

      gr.   Granules lying just within the nuclear membrane.
      n. m. Nuclear membrane.
      n. n. Nuclear network.
      Other lettering as in Figure 7.

PLATE IX.

Spicules.

Figure 1.—*Leucosolenia lucasi.*

      a.   Triradiate.
      b.   Quadriradiates; facial view, the apical ray represented as seen in optical section at its base.
      b.'   Quadriradiate; side view, showing the apical ray (*a. r.*) in full length, the three facial rays being broken off short.
      c.   Oxeotes.

Figure 2.—*Leucosolenia stolonifer.*

      b.   Quadriradiates; facial view, the apical ray represented as seen in optical section at its base.
      b.'   Quadriradiates; side view, showing normal apical ray (*a. r.*) in full length.
      b."   Quadriradiates; side view, showing immensely hypertrophied apical ray (*a. r.*) in full length.
      c.   Oxeotes.

Figure 3.—*Leucosolenia dubia.*
    a. Triradiates.
    a.' Strongly sagittal triradiate (abnormal).
    b. Quadriradiate; facial view, the apical ray represented as seen in optical section at its base.
    c. Oxeotes.

Figure 4.—*Leucosolenia cavata.*
    a. Triradiates.
    b. Quadriradiate; facial view, the apical ray represented as seen in optical section at its base.
    c. Oxeotes.

Figure 5.—*Leucosolenia stipitata.*
    Triradiates from the body of the sponge.

NOTE.—The figures are all drawn to the same scale, with Zeiss's *camera lucida*, and multiplied by about 260 diameters. After the drawings were completed it was found that the camera employed caused a certain amount of distortion; this, however, only affects the largest spicules to any perceptible degree, causing some of the rays to be unduly elongated. As full descriptions and measurements of the spicules are given in the text it is hoped that the error thus introduced will not cause any serious inconvenience.

PLATE X.

Spicules.

Figure 1.— *Leucosolenia pelliculata* (Specimen A).
    a. Triradiates.
    a.' Sagittal oscular triradiate.
    b. Quadriradiates; facial view, the apical ray represented as seen in optical section at its base.
    b.' Quadriradiate; side view, showing the full length of the apical ray (*a. r.*), the facial rays being broken off short.
    b." Sagittal oscular quadriradiate; facial view, the apical ray represented as seen in optical section at its base.

Figure 2.—*Leucosolenia pelliculata.* (Specimen D.)
    Lettering as in Figure 1.

Figure 3.—*Leucosolenia pulcherrima.*
    a. Ordinary deep-lying triradiates.
    a.' Stout, curved dermal triradiates.

Figure 4.—*Leucosolenia ventricosa.*
    a. Triradiates of various sizes.
    b. Quadriradiates; facial view, the apical ray represented as seen in optical section at its base.
    c. Oxeote.

NOTE.—The note after the description of Plate IX. applies equally to this plate.

PLATE XI.
Spicules.

Figure 1.—*Leucosolenia protogenes.*
    Triradiates of different sizes.

Figure 2.—*Leucosolenia proxima.*
    Triradiates of different sizes.

Figure 3.—*Leucosolenia wilsoni.*
    Triradiates of different sizes.

Figure 4.—*Leucosolenia depressa.*
    a. Triradiates.
    b. Quadriradiates ; facial view, the apical ray represented as seen in optical section at its base.

Figure 5.—*Leucosolenia tripodifera.*
    a. Triradiates.
    a.' Dermal triradiate (tripod spicule), side view.
    b. Quadriradiates; facial view, the apical ray represented as seen in optical section at its base.
    b.' Quadriradiate; side view, showing the apical ray (*a. r.*) at full length; one of the facial rays is broken off and one represented as seen in optical section at its base.
    b." Quadriradiate; facial view, showing the whole of the much curved apical ray (*a. r.*).

NOTE. The note after the description of Plate IX. applies equally to this plate.

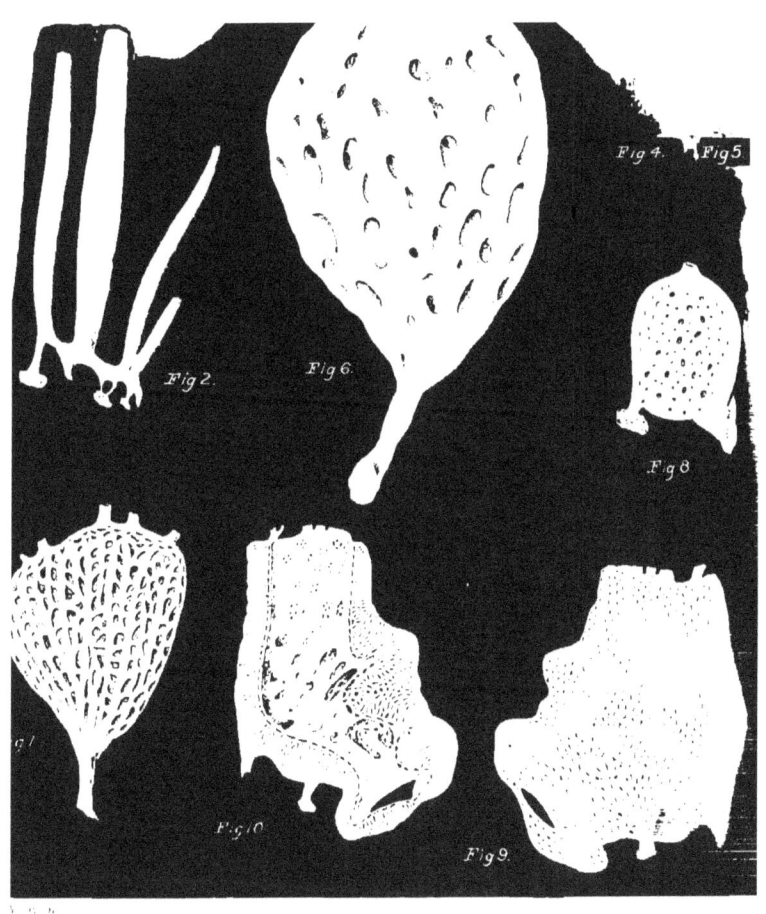

(1. Leucosolenia lucasi; 2. L. stolonifer; 3. L. dubia; 4,5,6. L. stipitata; 7. pulchet...; 8,9,10. L. ventricosa.)

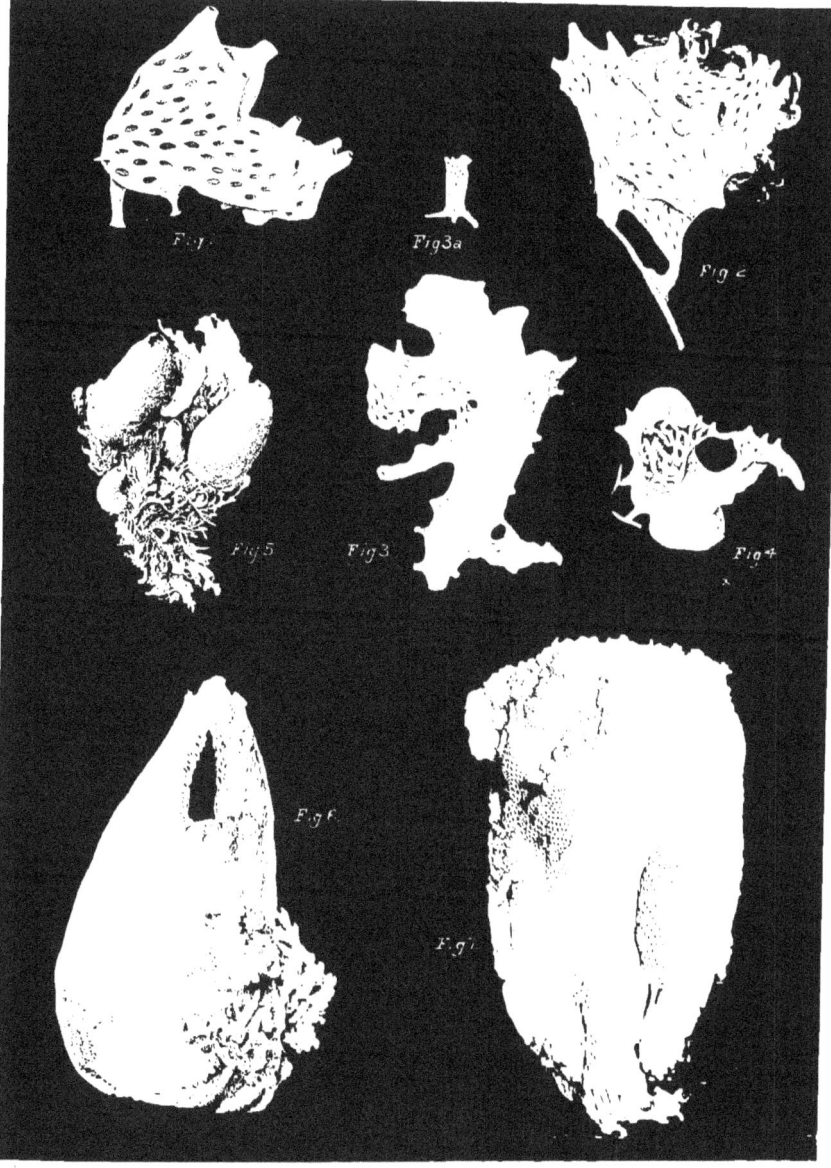

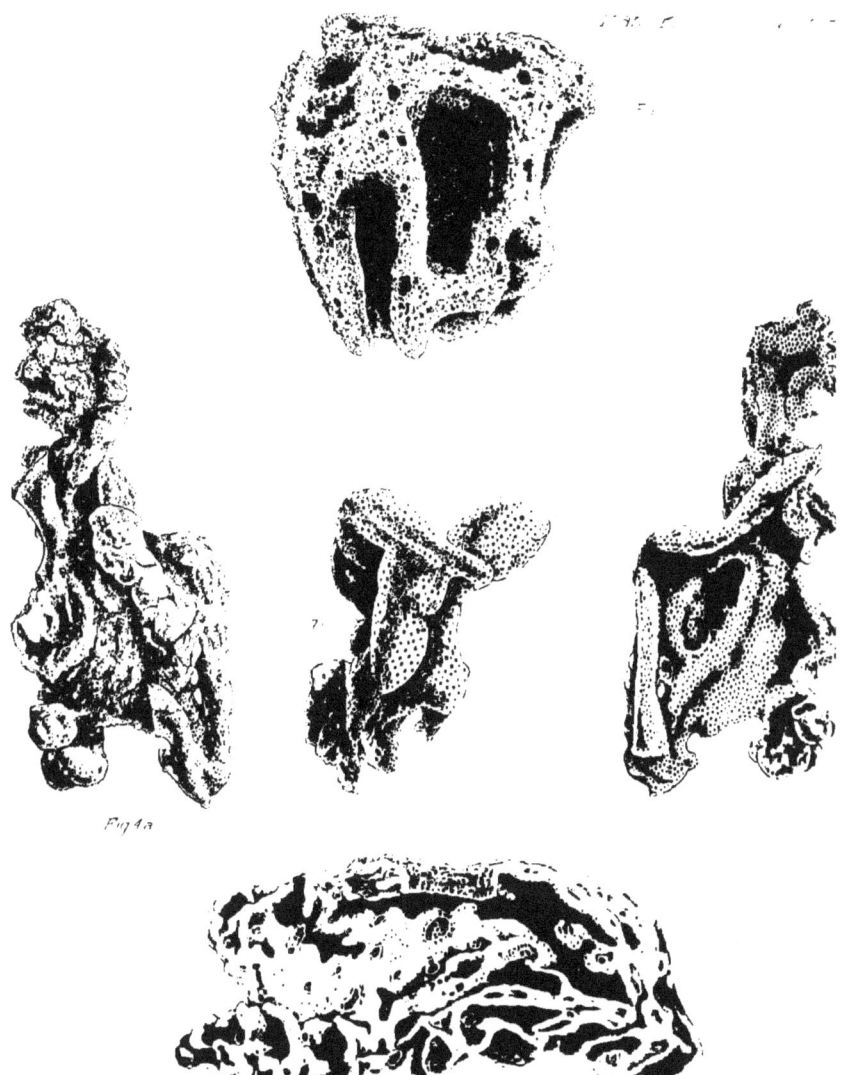

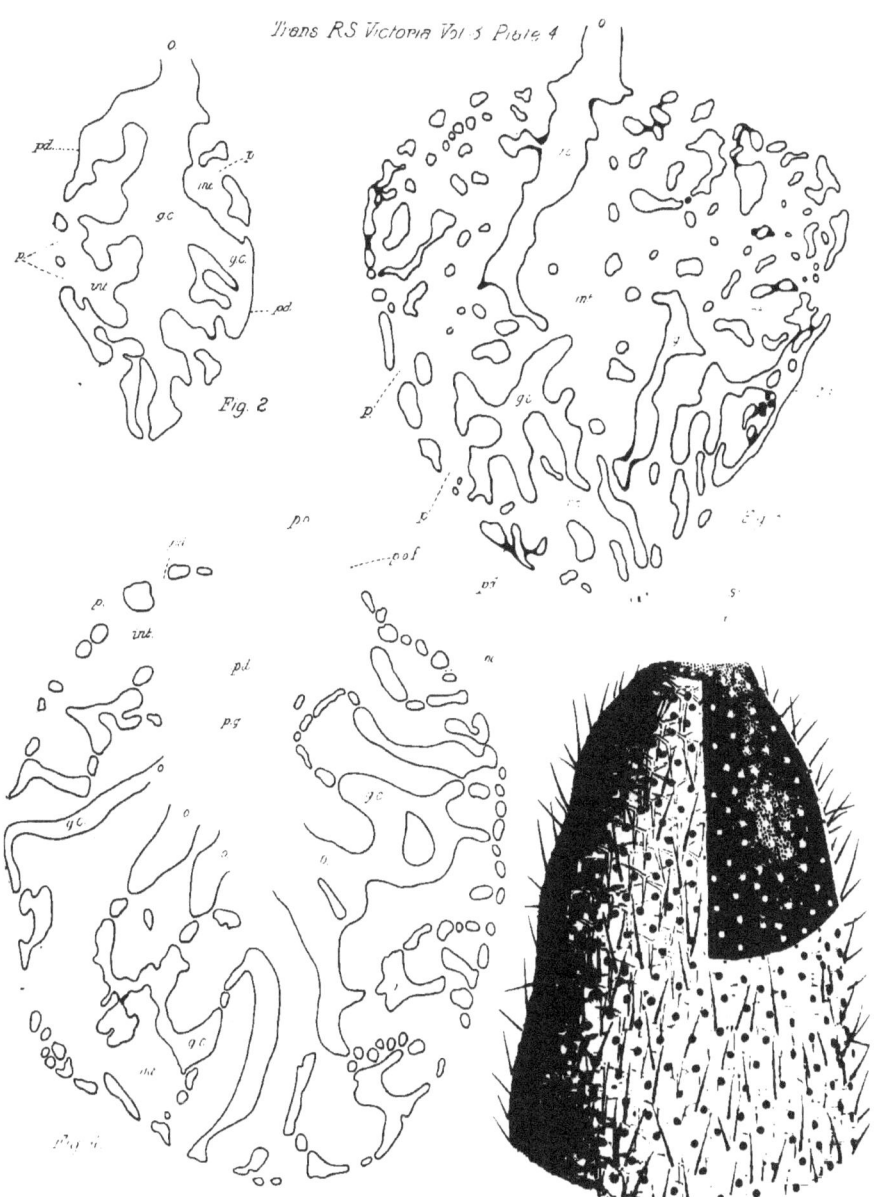

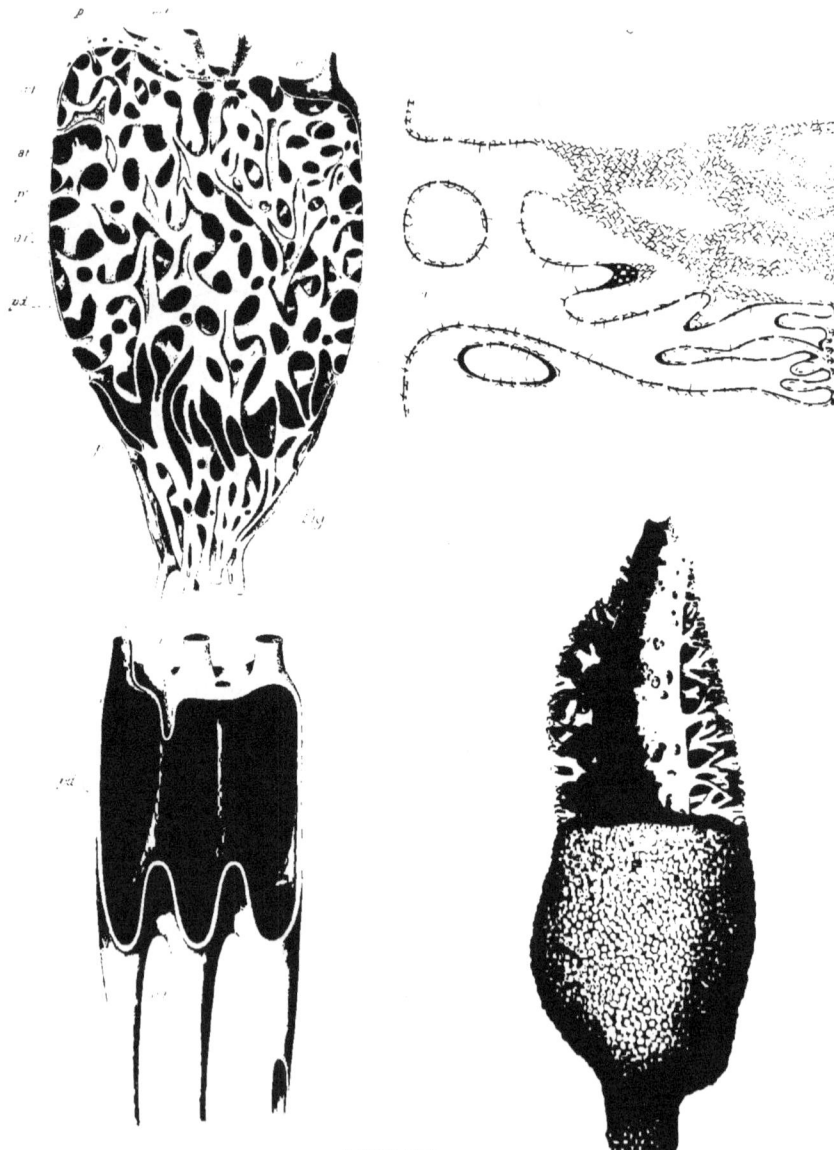

ANATOMY
(1.2. Leucosolenia cavata, 3.4 Leucosolenia...)

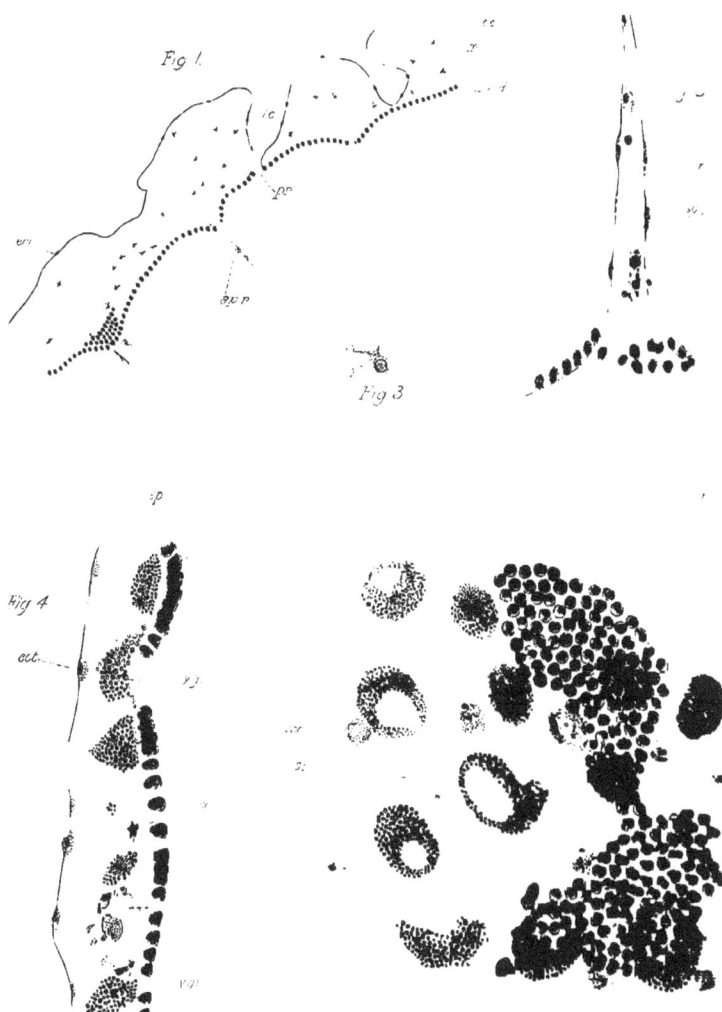

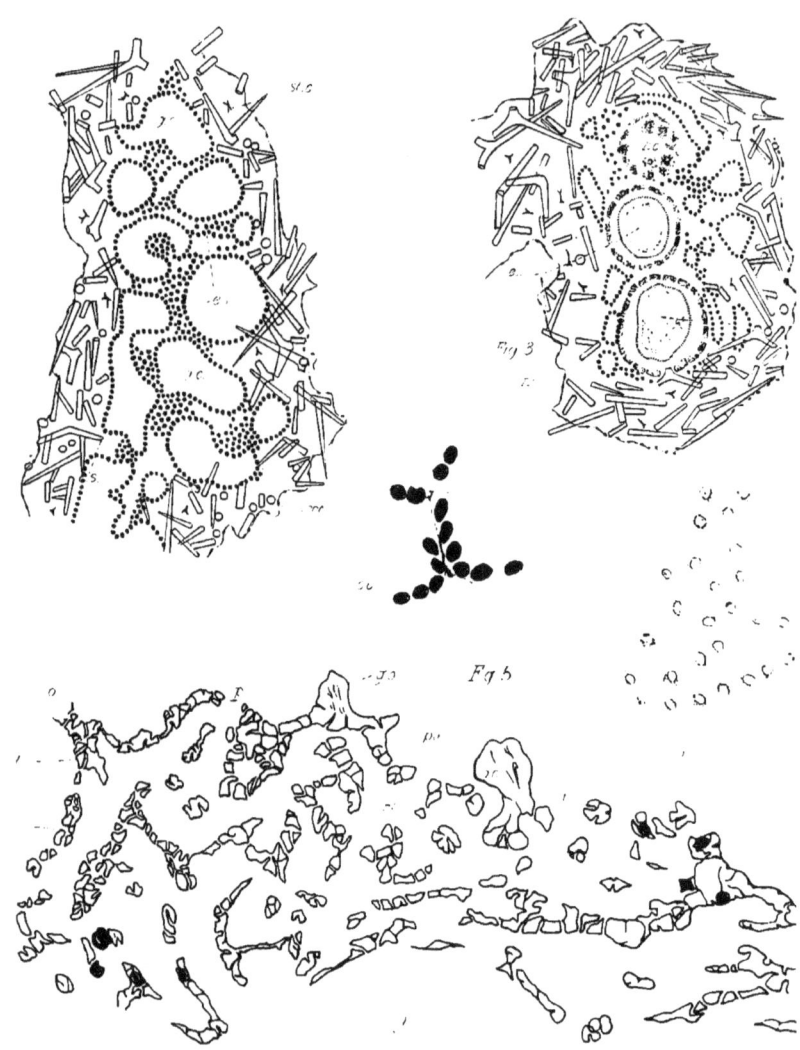

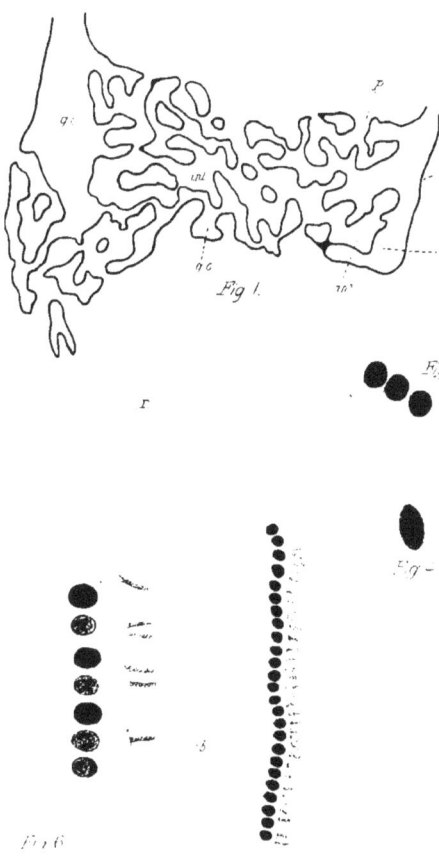

www.ingramcontent.com/pod-product-compliance
Lightning Source LLC
Chambersburg PA
CBHW031123160426
43192CB00008B/1090